THE SUNDAY SCHOOL
TEACHER'S GUIDE

The Sunday School Teacher's Guide

John Angell James

CountedFaithful

THE SUNDAY SCHOOL TEACHER'S GUIDE

First published in 1816
© Counted Faithful, 2025

COUNTED FAITHFUL
2 Drakewood Road
London SW16 5DT, UK

Website: https://www.countedfaithful.org

ISBN
Paperback: 978-1-78872-368-8
ePub: 978-1-78872-369-5
Kindle: 978-1-78872-370-1

Contents

Preface   7

Introduction – The History of the Sunday School System   11

1.   The Ultimate Object of Sunday School Instruction   31

2.   The Qualifications of Sunday School Teachers   43

3.   Directions as to the Duty of a Teacher   53

4.   The Duties of Teachers to Each Other   71

5.   The Temptations of Sunday School Teachers   81

6.   The Discouragements of Sunday School Teachers   87

7.   The Preservation of Zeal in Sunday School Teachers   95

8.   Motives to Diligence   101

Appendix

     A. Musical Performances at Sunday School
     Anniversaries   115

     B. Public Exhibitions of the Children   117

     C. Teaching Writing on the Sabbath   117

     D. Savings' Banks for Children   121

     E. The Results of Sunday School Teaching   123

A Memoir of Elizabeth Bales   125

Preface

THE design of the following work must secure the approbation of all who consider the present extent and increasing importance of the Sunday School system of instruction. We have arrived at that important era of the moral history of this country, when, by an unconstrained election, the lower classes of the community have chosen their better-instructed neighbours as the guardians of their children's minds and manners. It is an interesting fact, that the next generation of those who are to work in our manufactories, to labour in our fields, to minister about our persons, to defend our liberties, and who, according to their moral character, diffuse, through a thousand channels, the curses or the comforts of society, are voluntarily placed in our hands for the culture of their hearts and the formation of their manners; they are *en masse* looking up to us for instruction, and virtually saying, "Make us what you would have us to be." This is a circumstance of a most deeply interesting nature, and is worthy of the attention of the philanthropist, the patriot, and the Christian. It is a valuable and sacred deposit for which we are accountable both to heaven and earth; to the present and to every future generation of mankind.

Any effort therefore to guide the benevolence of those who have voluntarily undertaken the active duties of instruction deserves at least the acknowledgment due to good intentions, and this probably is the only debt which the author can justly claim of the public for this unostentatious little volume, the history of which is as follows. Having been repeatedly pressed to print a second edition of an address delivered to the Sunday School teachers of the Birmingham Union, the author was preparing to comply with the request, when it appeared to him that the subject might helpfully be dealt with more fully; and he resolved upon publishing a fuller account of the duties of the office, formed upon the basis of the original address. The fruit of his determination he now offers to the public.

He has thought fit to embody every sentiment and almost every expression of the address in the present volume, in order that those who desired the former might find in the latter, if they should be disposed to purchase it, the very object of their wishes.

Everything of a controversial nature has been carefully excluded, so that the book may be rendered acceptable to all religious denominations. If anyone should be disappointed in finding nothing said about the regulations of Sunday Schools, the author begs to observe that his object was with the moral and religious part of the institution, and not with its mechanism.

It is not improbable that in the estimation of some he may appear to have invested the institution with an undue degree of importance, and to have thrown upon the subject too much of the seriousness of religion and the solemn grandeur of eternity. To this, however, he cannot plead guilty, convinced as he is that the original design of Sunday Schools was religious instruction, and that their ultimate object should be the salvation of the immortal soul.

If any should think that, in reference to certain prevailing practices, the author fears where no fear is, he begs again to state that, as he considers the system of Sunday School education in the light of a religious institution, and is concerned that others should consider it so too, he feels a godly jealousy of everything likely to interfere with its efficiency in this high and sacred relation.

He acknowledges his peculiar obligations to the *Sunday School Repository* for information relating to the origin, progress, and improvements of the system.

The author now sends forth this unpretending production, conscious that it has many faults which have been multiplied by the frequent interruptions attendant upon the situation in which he is placed. Should it serve no other purpose than to provoke an abler pen, he will rejoice, when sinking in the shadow of his successor, that he has not laboured in vain.

– Introduction –

A Brief Account of the Origin, Progress, and Improvement of Sunday Schools

T O trace a mighty river to its source has ever been considered a sublime and worthy employment. It is pleasing to ascend its course from the point where it opens into the ocean, and becomes the inlet of wealth to an empire, until we arrive at the spot where it bubbles up a spring but just sufficient to irrigate the meadows of the neighbouring farm, and in descending to observe, as it receives the confluence of tributary waters, how it diffuses its benefits to those that dwell upon its banks. Still more engaging is the task, to trace the streams of Christian benevolence to their source, and contemplate the origin of those institutions which diffuse eternal blessings to immortal souls. For what is the Nile or the Niger, the Missouri, the Euphrates, the Thames, compared to the river of life? The smallest rivulet which flows into this celestial stream has more sublimity and importance than the mightiest rivers upon earth, and will be traced with the deepest interest upon the map of the Redeemer's kingdom millions of ages after the ocean itself shall have been for ever dissipated. Justly therefore may it be accounted an object worthy of our attention to trace, by a rapid survey, the origin, progress, and improvement of the Sunday School institution.

It is almost impossible for the greater part of those who are employed in diffusing the benefits of this admirable system to form an adequate idea of the extreme ignorance of the poor before its introduction. Except where a happy few of their children were gathered beneath the wings of some charitable institution, the great mass of their offspring grew up in the most deplorable ignorance. There were continually rising into life myriads of children of both sexes to whom the letters of the alphabet were mystic symbols, and every page of inspired or uninspired writ an insoluble wonder. And this was the least part of their calamity. Ignorance is the prolific mother of crimes and miseries. It is during a state of mental night that the worst vices of the human character steal from their coverts in the heart to prey upon the peace and comforts of society. To the children of the poor the Sabbath seemed to suspend the toils of the body, only to afford them greater leisure for effecting the ruin of their souls. They claimed the sacred hours as their own, and diligently employed them to aid their growth in wickedness. In the vicinity of every large town multitudes were to be seen practising every boyish sport; while others spread over the face of the country to commit depredations on orchards and gardens. In many places the farmer was detained from public worship to guard his property, or employed his servants in the task. People going to the house of God, not only had their minds disturbed, but received personal violence from numerous bands of those unhappy youths, the more desperate sometimes associating for the purpose of molesting those whom conscience led to worship in the meeting-house rather than the church. Thus every generation of the poor was growing up successively, without any general effort to instruct their ignorance, to check their violence, to repress their vices, or to form their manners.

In this state matters remained until God in his great goodness raised up a man whose memory innumerable multitudes will bless; and to whose name religion will assign a distinguished rank on the roll of benefactors of the human race, which she carefully preserves in the archives of the church. To the last moment of time, and through every age of eternity, Robert Raikes will be venerated as the father and founder of Sunday Schools, or at least as the person who made them known to the public. This illustrious man was a native of Gloucester, and was born in the year 1735. His heart was one of mercy's earthly temples; his benevolence was ardent and active. The first object which engaged his philanthropic exertions was the miserable situation of the prisoners confined for lesser crimes in the county jail, for whose instruction and reformation he made a noble and successful struggle. The circumstances which led to the institution of Sunday Schools shall be stated in his own words. In a letter to a gentleman who had applied to him for the particulars of the nature and origin of his plan, he thus writes:

"Some business leading me one morning into the suburbs of the city, where the lowest of the people (who are principally employed in the pin manufactory) reside, I was struck with concern at seeing a group of children, wretchedly ragged, at play in the street. I asked an inhabitant whether those children belonged to that part of the town, and lamented their misery and idleness. 'Ah! sir,' said the woman to whom I was speaking, 'could you take a view of this part of the town on Sunday, you would be shocked indeed; for then the street is filled with multitudes of these wretches, who, released on that day from their employment, spend their time in noise and riot, playing at chuck, and cursing and swearing in a manner so horrid as to convey to any serious mind an idea of hell rather than of any other place. We have a worthy clergyman,' said she, 'minister of our parish, who has put some of them to school; but upon the Sabbath they are all given up to follow their inclinations without restraint, as their parents, totally abandoned themselves, have no idea of instilling into the minds of their children principles to which they themselves are strangers.'

"This conversation suggested to me, that it would at least be a harmless attempt, if it were productive of no good, should some little plan be formed to check this deplorable profanation of the Sabbath. I then inquired of the woman if there were any decent well-disposed women in the neighbourhood who kept schools for teaching to read. I was presently directed to four. To these I applied, and made an agreement with them to receive as many children as I should send on the Sunday, whom they were to instruct in reading and the church catechism. For this I engaged to pay them a shilling for their day's employment. The women seemed pleased with the proposal. I then waited on the clergyman before-mentioned, and imparted to him my plan. He was so much satisfied with the idea that he engaged to lend his assistance by going round to the schools on a Sunday afternoon, to examine the progress that was made, and to enforce order and decorum among such a set of little heathens.

"This sir, is the commencement of the plan. It is now about three years since we began; and I could wish you were here to make inquiry into the effect. A woman who lives in a lane where I had fixed a school told me, some time ago, that the place was like a heaven upon Sundays compared with what it used to be. The numbers who have learned to read and say their catechism are so great that I am astonished at it. Upon the Sunday afternoon the mistresses take their scholars to church, a place into which neither they nor their ancestors ever entered with a view to the glory of God. But, what is yet more extraordinary, within this month these little ragamuffins have, in great numbers, taken it into their heads to frequent the early morning prayers, which are held every morning at the cathedral at seven o'clock. I believe there were near fifty this morning. They assemble at the house of one of the mistresses, and walk before her to church, two and two, in as much order as a company of soldiers. I am generally at church, and after service they all come round me to 'make their bow,' and if any animosities have arisen to make their complaint. The great principle I inculcate is to be kind and good-natured to each other; not to provoke one another; to be dutiful to their parents; not to offend God by cursing and swearing; and such little plain precepts as all may comprehend. As my profession is that of a printer, I have printed a little book, which I give out to them; and some friends of mine, subscribers to the *Society for the Promotion of Christian Knowledge*, sometimes make me a present of a parcel of Bibles, Testaments, etc, which I distribute as rewards to the deserving. The success that has attended this scheme has induced one or two of my friends to adopt the plan, and set up Sunday Schools in other parts of the city; and now a whole parish has taken up the object; so that I flatter myself that in time the good effects will appear so conspicuous as to become generally adopted. The number of children at present thus engaged on the Sabbath is between two and three hundred, and they are increasing every week, as the benefit is universally seen. I have endeavoured to engage the clergy of my acquaintance that reside in their parishes. One has entered into the scheme with great fervour; and it was in order to excite others to follow the example that I inserted in my paper the paragraph which I suppose you saw copied into the London papers. I cannot express to you the pleasure I often receive in discovering genius and innate good dispositions among this little multitude. It is like a miniature study in human nature. I have often too the satisfaction of receiving thanks from parents for the reformation they perceive in their children. Often have I given them kind admonitions, which I always do in the mildest and gentlest manner. The going among them, doing them little kindnesses, distributing trifling rewards, and ingratiating myself with them, I hear, have given me an ascendency greater than I ever could have imagined: for I am told by their mistresses that they are very much afraid of my displeasure. If you ever pass through Gloucester, I shall be happy to pay my respects to you, and to show you the effects of this effort at civilisation. If the glory of God be promoted in any, even the smallest degree, society must reap some benefit. If good seed be sown in the mind at an early period of human life, though it shows itself not again for many years, it may please God, at some future period, to cause it to spring up, and to bring forth a plenteous harvest."

It appears that Mr Raikes' effort commenced about the close of the year 1781, or the beginning of 1782. His example was immediately copied by some of his friends, and the system began to extend itself in the city of Gloucester. Having tried the experiment for more than a year, he determined to invite public attention to a scheme which he perceived to be attended with so many benefits. For this purpose he inserted a paragraph in a weekly newspaper, of which he was the editor and printer.

The following is a copy of this important and modest notice from the *Gloucester Journal*, November 3, 1783.

"Some of the clergy in different parts of this country, bent upon attempting reform among the children of the lower class, are establishing Sunday Schools for rendering the Lord's Day subservient to the ends of instruction, which has hitherto been prostituted to bad purposes. Farmers and other inhabitants of the towns and villages complain that they receive more injury in their property on the Sabbath than all the week besides; this in a great measure proceeds from the lawless state of the younger class, who are allowed to run wild on that day, free from every restraint. To remedy this evil, persons duly qualified are employed to instruct those that cannot read; and those that may have learnt to read are taught the catechism, and conducted to church. By thus keeping their minds engaged, the day passes profitably, and not disagreeably. In those parishes where this plan has been adopted, we are assured that the behaviour of the children is greatly civilised. The barbarous ignorance in which they had before lived being in some degree dispelled, they begin to give proofs that those persons are mistaken, who consider the lower orders of mankind as incapable of improvement, and therefore think an attempt to reclaim them impracticable, or at least not worth the trouble." [1]

Mr Raikes' statement of the good effects of his schools was not permitted by Him who watches every event, to float unobserved to oblivion, nor indeed was it likely to do so. It caught the attention of a gentleman in Lancashire before alluded to, who wrote immediately to him, and received the letter already given. By permission of its author, this letter was printed in the *Gentleman's Magazine* for 1784. (Volume 51, page 410.) Through the medium of this publication, the plan was laid before thousands of the most intelligent members of society in the kingdom; and Mr Raikes soon had to answer the inquiries of other correspondents anxious to gain information on this new and important subject.

The scheme began now to be very generally known and adopted. Christians of all denominations, wondering that it should never have been devised before, seemed determined to repair, as much as possible, the mischief of past neglect, by applying with the utmost diligence the benefits of this new discovery in the world of morals and religion.

Several public-spirited gentlemen in the metropolis, perceiving that the system would be greatly aided by the establishment of

---

1. The *Gentleman's Magazine* for February 1837, contains a memoir of the Rev David Williams, of Heytesbury, in which the following sentences occur: "In a conversation with the then Mr Stork, the vicar of Cheselden, and his nephew of the same name the incumbent of a parish in Gloucester, he (the Rev David Williams) suggested the introduction of Sunday Schools as a means of preventing the misemployment of the Sabbath by young people of both sexes. The uncle adopted the suggestion at Cheselden, the nephew at Gloucester, when the zeal, activity, and munificence of Mr Raikes, the banker, gave him the universal credit of having been the founder of Sunday Schools. *Tulit alter honores.* The first experiment had been made in the curacies of David Williams, in North Wiltshire, and was subsequently continued in all the parishes of which he had the charge." *Ed.*

a society which should combine the patronage and energies of all denominations of Christians, held a preparatory meeting August 30, 1785, to take into consideration the propriety of forming a society, for establishing and supporting Sunday Schools for the instruction of poor children in different parts of the kingdom. In consequence of a resolution then passed, a public meeting was held on the 7th of September, and an institution formed, bearing the title of *A Society for the Support and Encouragement of Sunday Schools in the Different Counties in England.* This establishment was exceedingly beneficial to the growing cause. By the respectability of its members, it increased the public confidence; by their talents it enlightened the public mind; by their activity it stimulated the public zeal; and by their property it assisted the public expenditure for the object.

It was an object of importance with the committee of the *Sunday School Society* to engage the co-operation of episcopal authority within the pale of the established religion of the country; and it must be spoken to the honour of the bishops, that they promptly came forward and cast the weight of their mitres into the scale of this good cause. Among the dignitaries of the church who patronised the plan, the Bishops of Salisbury and Llandaff, and the Deans of Canterbury and Lincoln, obtained a conspicuous place by their zeal and talents. So rapidly did the flame spread through the country, that by the close of 1786, it is conjectured not less than 250,000 children were every Sunday receiving instruction.

The schools were at first universally conducted by hired teachers. This entailed a load of pecuniary difficulty upon the plan, which, had it not been removed, would have considerably retarded its progress, and consequently diminished its usefulness. The *Sunday School Society* alone expended during the first sixteen years of its existence no less than four thousand pounds in the salaries of teachers. And this was not the least evil attending upon purchased labour. Hireling teachers can scarcely be expected to possess either the zeal or ability of those who now engage in the work from motives of pure benevolence. Gratuitous instruction was an astonishing improvement of the system, though it does not appear to have entered into the views of its benevolent author. "If we were asked," says a writer in the *Sunday School Repository*, "whose name stood next to that of

Robert Raikes in the annals of Sunday Schools, we should say, the person who first came forward, and *voluntarily* offered his exertions, his time, and his talents, to the instruction of the young and the poor; since an imitation of his example has been the great cause of the present flourishing state of these institutions, and of all that future additional increase which may be reasonably anticipated." At what precise period this was first introduced, does not appear, or where it commenced; so that the award of this second honour is reserved for the decision of the last day. About the year 1800 the plan became very general throughout the kingdom.

The improvement in the mode of popular education, introduced by Dr Bell and Mr Lancaster, must be considered as forming another era in the history of Sunday Schools, by affording new facilities to the business of instruction. And the advantages derived from these useful systems does not merely consist in the servile imitation of all their arrangements, but in demonstrating to the world more clearly than was ever shown before, that education is an art susceptible of indefinite improvement, and in exciting an ardour before unknown, to carry it on to perfection.

The institution of Sunday Schools was now become universal in this kingdom. Every city and every town had warmly espoused the cause. Still there was one thing wanting to raise the system to the highest degree of efficiency, and that was union. In every possible application of the sentiment, union is power. Reasoning upon the general principle, many were led to conclude that great benefits would result to this particular case, from an association of counsel and energy. After much private intercourse on this subject, between many people in London, a public meeting was held on July 13, 1803, in the school rooms belonging to Surrey Chapel, and the *Sunday School Union* was then formed. The design of this association is thus announced in its own regulations:

"The objects of this Union are, 1st, To stimulate and encourage each other in the religious instruction of the young. 2ndly, By mutual communication to improve the methods of instruction. 3rdly, To promote the opening of new schools. 4thly, To print books, etc, suitable for Sunday Schools, at a cheap rate. 5thly, To correspond with ministers and others in the United Kingdom and abroad. 6thly, To promote the formation of country Unions, which are expected regularly to report to this Society; and are allowed to purchase its publications at reduced prices."

This new society commenced its operations with no less prudence than vigour. Carefully abstaining from even the appearance of a desire to interfere with the private management of any of the associated schools, it aimed to diffuse new life and energy through them all. One of its first objects was the compilation of a new spelling book, more adapted to moral and religious instruction than any they could find already in existence. This production reflects no small degree of credit on its industrious compilers. The next object of the committee was to ascertain, by an extensive correspondence, what parts of the country were most destitute of schools. Finding, in many places, that the advantages of the system were greatly diminished by the want of method and order which prevailed in the schools, they published in 1806, *A Plan for the Formation and Regulation of Sunday Schools.*

The example of the metropolis was soon imitated in many of the large towns and several counties. Unions were formed in different parts of the kingdom, from which the happiest effects have resulted; among which may be reckoned the establishment of new schools in neglected parts of large towns, and amidst the darkness of benighted villages; a fresh excitement given to those employed in the work of tuition; the diffusion of Christian affection; and in some instances a great improvement in the mode of instruction. The formation of the *Sunday School Union* must, therefore, be regarded as an event of vast importance to the success of this valuable scheme.

It must be acknowledged however that in some few instances, the benefits of these regional Unions have not been without an admixture of evil. A disposition to conceited self-importance, to form factions, and to a turbulent spirit and independence, has occasionally, though it is hoped but rarely, manifested itself, which has led to the breaking up of the association, and extended its mischiefs to the churches to which the schools belonged. These instances have formed the exceptions, not the rule.

In an account like the present, the establishment of the *Scotch Sabbath Evening Schools* ought not to be omitted. The children of the poor, so far as common education is concerned, are all taught to read in the parochial schools, which are established in that enlightened country. Still, however, as it respects the observance of the Sabbath, and the more direct business of religious instruction, like the children in England, they are left of course to the care of their parents; multitudes of whom, indifferent to the welfare of their own souls, feel no concern for the salvation of their offspring. Observing and commiserating the condition of these neglected youth, who in great numbers spent the Sabbath, and especially the Sabbath evenings, in profanity and vice, the friends of religion formed the pious resolution of collecting them together on the Lord's Day evenings, for the purpose of imparting religious knowledge. They assemble at six o'clock and are dismissed about eight; during which time every effort is made to instruct them in the way of eternal salvation, and to urge them forward in the path of life. How desirable is it that the plan should pass the Tweed, and be adopted in England! There is one class of youth to whom it might become an incalculable blessing: I mean the older boys and girls who have just left our schools, and who are generally considered as gone beyond our care. Thus abandoned by us, it is too commonly the case that they lose all the little impression they have received while under our instruction. Could they be collected together on a Sabbath evening, to be taught by the senior and more pious members of our churches, who would interest themselves in their welfare, what a blessing might be expected to accrue!

Wales at a very early period in the history of Sunday Schools entered with eagerness into the scheme, and adorned her romantic and picturesque valleys with numerous Schools for the instruction of the poor.

And here it is but justice to the Sunday School as an institution, although by some it may be accounted a digression, to assert its claims to the high honour of giving birth to the most sublime and efficient society ever formed by man, or blessed by God, for promoting the interests of genuine Christianity. Every reader will anticipate the name of the *British and Foreign Bible Society*. The honour of giving rise to this mighty combination of wealth, zeal and talent is more worth contending for than the highest place in the roll of monarchs, conquerors or philosophers. Newton, the greatest discoverer in natural philosophy, if he be acquainted with what is done on earth, would cheerfully resign all the glory of his peerless works, for the brighter honour of having originated this great and godly scheme.

By means of Sunday School education in Wales, the number of readers increased far beyond any supply of Welsh Bibles which could be obtained. This induced the indefatigable Mr Charles of Bala to undertake a journey to London for the purpose of soliciting a private subscription from his friends, to defray the expense of printing a new edition. In the course of conversation on this subject, at a committee meeting of the *Religious Tract Society*, a thought came into the mind of the Rev Joseph Hughes, (a thought which darted as one of the brightest beams from the fountain of light and life above, and for which millions through eternity will bless his name,) that a little more exertion than was requisite for supplying the Principality with the Scriptures, might found an institution that should go on increasing its funds, and extending its operations, until not only the British dominions, but the whole world, should be furnished with the Word of God. Such was the origin of a society which is the glory of our own age and nation, and will one day be acknowledged as a blessing to all ages and all nations. I have no need to trace the proposal further than to say that it was warmly embraced by the gentlemen present, and steps were immediately taken to give it efficiency. My only object in referring to the *British and Foreign Bible Society*, was to show its pedigree, and claim it as the blooming daughter of the Sunday School institution.

The cause which originated it still supports it. For in most cases Sunday School teachers are among the keenest to see Bibles distributed widely.

Ireland, geographically separated from us only by the narrow channel of the Irish Sea, but far remote from England as to the moral and religious state of her inhabitants, begins to share in the advantages of this beneficial plan. In the year 1810, the *Hibernian Sunday School Society* was formed, which was immediately cherished by extensive patronage, and has already been exceedingly useful in scattering the rays of heavenly light over the gloom which has long enveloped the lower classes of the community in that country so neglected, though so interesting.

In tracing the growth of the Sunday School institution it would be an unpardonable omission to pass by in silence that noble ramification of it, the instruction of adults. A few years ago, had anyone proposed such a design, a thousand voices would have exclaimed, in a strain somewhat similar to that of the wondering and doubting Nicodemus, "How can a man be taught when he is old?" But this is the age of a daring and restless benevolence, which no exertions can weary, and no difficulties can appal. The first scion was planted by Mr Charles upon the mountains of Wales in the summer of 1811. "God prepared room before it, and caused it to take deep root; the hills were covered with the shadow of it, and the boughs thereof were like goodly cedars." The account of his commencement and success shall be given in his own words:

"My maxim has been, for many years past, to aim at great things; but if I cannot accomplish great things, to do what I can, and be thankful for the least success, and still to follow on, without being discouraged at the day of small things, or by unexpected reverses. For many years I have laid it down as a maxim to guide me, never to give up a place in despair of success. If one way does not succeed, new means must be tried; and if I see no increase this year, perhaps I may the next. I almost wish to blot out the word *impossible* from my vocabulary, and obliterate it from the minds of my brethren. We had no particular school for the instruction of adults exclusively, until the summer of 1811; but many attended the Sunday Schools with the children in different parts of the country prior to that time. What induced me first to think of establishing such an institution was the aversion I found in the adults to associate with the children in their schools. The first attempt succeeded wonderfully, and far beyond my most sanguine expectations. The report of the success of this school soon spread over the country, and in many places the illiterate adults began to call for instruction. In one county, after a public address had been delivered to them on the subject, the adult poor, even the aged, flocked to the Sunday School in crowds; and the shopkeepers could not immediately supply them with an adequate number of spectacles. Our schools in general are kept in our chapels: in some districts, where there are no chapels, farmers, in the summer time, lend their barns. The adults and children are sometimes in the same room, but placed in different parts of it. When their attention is gained and fixed, they soon learn; their age makes no difference, if they are able, by the help of glasses, to see the letters. As the adults have no time to lose, we endeavour (before they can read) to instruct them without delay, in the first principles of Christianity. We select short portions of Scripture, comprising the leading doctrines and repeat them to the learners, until they can retain them in their memories, and which they are to repeat the next time we meet."

Thus commenced that excellent institution, which is imparting the elements of knowledge, and the benefits of religious instruction to thousands who have passed the meridian of life; which in many cases by teaching the aged to read seems to add a lengthened twilight to their day of grace; and by revealing to them the things that belong to their peace, just as they are about to be hid from their eyes, accomplishes the words of inspiration, "In the evening-tide it shall be light."

Soon after this time, as if the plan had been wafted by the Severn, and thence received by the Avon, it appeared in the city of Bristol. The individual destined to the high honour of establishing it there was a man of obscure and humble origin. The rays of spiritual light do not always strike first on the tops of the highest mountains. Men in less elevated stations have often been employed as the almoners of the divine bounty. The apostle, referring to the first preachers of the Gospel, could say, "Ye see your calling, brethren, how that not many wise men after the flesh, not many mighty, not many noble; but God hath chosen the foolish things of the world to confound the wise; and God hath chosen the weak things of the world to confound the things that are mighty." At the second anniversary of the *Bristol Auxiliary Bible Society*, among other intelligence communicated to the meeting, a letter from Keynsham was read, which contained the following sentence: "We have been necessarily obliged to omit a great number of poor inhabitants who could not read, and therefore are not likely to be benefitted by the possession of a Bible." This statement reached the heart of an individual present, by the name of William Smith. To be deprived of the inspired volume by inability to peruse it, appeared to him worse than for a man to be dying of the plague, through ignorance of the way of applying a remedy which was within his reach. His benevolent mind meditated upon their situation. He longed to relieve them, but scarcely dared to hope that the case admitted of relief. In this dilemma he consulted Stephen Prust, a merchant whose name stands high in the long list of Bristol philanthropists. The object of his inquiry was to ascertain whether it was possible to teach the ignorant part of the adult poor to read. It is of immense importance, that when the seed of benevolence begins to germinate, it should be cherished by the genial influence of a kindly atmosphere; a nipping frost at that critical juncture would cause it to perish in its bud. In the advice, patronage and support of Mr Prust the scheme of William Smith met the sunshine which it needed. Upon his plan he slept not a second night; and after he had received the promise of his generous friend to assist him in the undertaking, before he commenced his exertions, he was employed the next day in collecting subscriptions for the *Bible Association*, and whenever he met with people who could not read, he asked them whether they would like to learn if a school should be opened. Many embraced the offer with expressions of pleasure, and their names were taken down. Two rooms were immediately obtained, and the work of instruction commenced. So little could the ardour of Smith endure delay, that in nineteen days after he had disclosed his mind to Mr Prust, the school was opened with eleven men and ten women. The number rapidly increased until, a few weeks after, some active friends to the cause of religion and humanity met the founder of the new institution, and formed themselves into a society, bearing the title of *An Institution for Instructing Adult Persons to Read the Holy Scriptures*. The society continued to attract the attention, and engage the support, of Christians of all denominations; and at length received a most valuable accession in the active co-operation of Dr Pole, a physician in connection with the *Society of Friends*. Within the period of two years the society admitted 1508 scholars, in addition to the 276 who were taught by schools belonging to several dissenting congregations.[2]

Before I pass on from the successful results of William Smith's exertions in Bristol, it should be stated that, although his commencement was subsequent to Mr Charles' labours in Wales, he had at the time no knowledge of his precursor's noble career; the Fountain of all good thus causing the stream of his mercy to break forth in two distant places almost simultaneously.

2. See *A History of the Origin and Progress of Adult Schools*, by Thomas Pole.

It was not likely that this new light, kindled by Charles and Smith, would remain long unobserved. It was seen and admired from afar. Generous and noble-spirited men in different parts of the kingdom, ever watching for new methods of benefitting their fellow-men, hailed the beaming signal with delight, and like the eastern Magi, followed its directions, and flocked to the brightness of its rising. Schools multiplied everywhere, until, at the present time, they are to be found in almost every considerable town in the country.

The next event in the order of time of importance in the history of Sunday Schools is of a literary nature. The press is one of the best friends to the interest of man; and one of the most important auxiliaries to the cause of God. If, like the other gifts of heaven, it has been sometimes abused; if it has been pressed into the ranks of infidelity and cruelty; still, under the direction of holier and wiser minds, it has, after such abuse of its powers, turned with indignation upon its own work, repaired the mischief it has done, and demolishing the refuges of lies together with the habitations of cruelty, erected upon their ruins the temple of truth and the throne of mercy. The press has befriended the Sunday School system in many ways. I now select only one instance, but one of considerable importance; the *Sunday School Repository*, which commenced in January, 1813. This valuable work is calculated at once to interest, instruct, and excite. It should be circulated through every school, and read by every teacher. Already it has laid before the public a mass of most the valuable information, and directed upon the Sunday School institution a stream of light which has revealed its magnitude and its beauty much more clearly than they were generally seen before. And in order to render it still more useful, everyone who has much experience in the business of instruction, and is possessed of an ability to communicate his knowledge to others, should consider his talents as put under requisition for its support. It might become of immense importance to the great cause. If a good digest were made of all the information of this nature that could be obtained, it would exhibit the operations of the whole Christian world in this respect, and so form a sort of panorama, in which, as in one connected and beautiful picture, the whole circle of Sunday School operations might be contemplated wherever it is read.

I now turn our attention from our own country to the adoption and progress of the plan in other quarters of the globe. A few years ago the *British and Foreign Bible Society*, as with the wings of the angel in the Apocalypse, flew across the Atlantic, and lighted on the shores of a country which presented a new world to the operations of religion no less than those of commerce and conquest. America, deriving from England everything which she possesses of value in religion, has cherished in her bosom this glorious institution ever since its arrival on her shores, but has at length found, as we have done, that ignorance prescribes limits to its operations, which nothing but the Sunday School system can break down. The western breeze lately brought to us the request, "Complete the mercy you have begun in giving us the *Bible Society* by sending us the Sunday School institution." The call was promptly obeyed, and the eastern wind, which some say blows no good to anyone, took back various publications relating both to children's and adult schools. Letters have been received, one or two extracts from which will record the establishment of the institution in the United States.

The earliest intimation of its having claimed the attention of the Americans was received in a letter from Divie Bethune, of New York, to Mr Prust, dated July 13, 1814. The former, alluding to a present of a copy of Dr Pole's *History of Adult Schools* which he had received from Mr Prust, says, "Mrs Bethune, and about twenty other ladies have petitioned the corporation of this city to grant them the use of a building erected for a house of industry. Mrs B___ says she is of the opinion that an adult school may very properly be attached to such an institution."

The first intelligence of the establishment of a school in Philadelphia is contained in a letter from Miss S Whitehead to Mr Bethune, dated March 23, 1815, which is as follows:

"I had several extracts from Dr Pole's work inserted in the *Religious Remembrancer*, a weekly paper of our city, and the subject excited universal attention; the Freemasons have taken it up; and at a general meeting it was proposed and carried unanimously, that several schools should be established and held in the Grand Lodge in Chestnut Street. There is no doubt that all the different lodges belonging to the fraternity will take up the subject, and that it will extend over the whole Union. One of the officers gave me this information. Mr Thomas Bradford commenced a school in the jail last Sabbath-day. Several pious female friends of mine propose shortly to commence one in the south end of the city, and thus you see how great a matter a little fire kindleth."

The next account was from Mr Bethune to Mr Prust, dated New York, June 10, 1815:

"It will be gratifying to you to learn, that your transmission of the report of the adult schools has been the means of awakening towards this object a great attention here. The loss of our valued mother, it appears, a gracious God is pleased in part to make up to society, by giving health and zeal to her daughter, Mrs Bethune, to follow her steps. The little school begun by her on reading Dr Pole's *History*, which you sent me, has succeeded astonishingly. She and my two daughters, assisted by a female friend, teach on Sunday mornings. It consists of between eighty and ninety learners; and their Bible class now able to read consists of forty-seven scholars."

It must be recorded to the honour of the female sex, that the first exertions in both these cities were made by them. And by a general survey of the Christian world, it would seem as if, conscious that the woman was "first in the transgression," they resolved she should not be the last in endeavouring to diffuse the blessings of salvation. In a letter from Mrs Bethune to Mr Prust, we have the following account of the formation of the first Sunday School for children which was ever established in the New World:

"Dear Sir,
"New York, January 24, 1816.
"I cannot resist the desire I feel to employ my pen in thanking you for your presents to myself and my children, of so many interesting publications; from which, I trust, we have derived both pleasure and profit. I believe I cannot express my gratitude in a way better suited to your liberal soul, than by giving you an account of a meeting held in this city today. Mr B___ published one of your letters in one of our daily papers: I lent the different publications relative to Sunday Schools to a number of our friends, and was in hopes the gentlemen would have come forward in the business; but after waiting a number of weeks, I conversed with several of my own sex, who expressed

a wish to unite with me in a *Female Sunday School Union*. Accordingly we called a meeting of the female members of all denominations, who met today in the lecture-room of one of our churches; and although the notice was not so general as intended, several hundreds were present. Dr R___ opened the meeting with a very appropriate prayer. When he withdrew, the ladies were pleased to call me to the chair. I addressed the meeting in a few words stating for what purpose their company was requested; the great need of such an institution, where numbers of one sex were training for the gallows and state prisons, and of the other for prostitution; likewise the great want of religious instruction in our small schools: the parents of children attending such, not having time to teach them, would probably avail themselves of Sunday Schools if within their reach. In order to stimulate them to so good a work, I said I would read them several extracts from British publications, which would show them how much the Lord had blessed such institutions in the Old World, and concluded by humbly hoping that He would extend the blessing to His hand-maidens in their attempts to train up a seed to serve Him in the New World.

"I may venture to affirm there was not a dry eye in the room, and tears flowed copiously down the cheeks of many. A committee was appointed of one or two from each denomination to prepare a constitution and set of rules, to be laid before the society at a meeting in a week's time."

In a letter from Mr Bethune, dated New York, February 4, 1816, we learn what was the result of this noble exertion of female piety and zeal.

"This city is in a stir throughout, a strong interest awakened and great exertions commenced for the instruction on Sabbath days of children and adults. Mrs B___ has written to you an account of the first meeting of ladies: a week later the second meeting was held; and so great was the crowd of ladies pressing forward, that the company had to adjourn from a lecture-room to a church.

"Next Sabbath, I believe, was appointed for the commencement of the work of teaching; the zeal of three of the congregations, however, led them to begin today. Mrs B___ visited these schools, which, with a school of black adults, taught by my family, make up one hundred and thirty-six scholars. I presume the number next Lord's Day will amount to one thousand in all the schools. I believe the gentlemen are mustering their numbers, to follow the example of the ladies, and to take charge of the adults and children of their own sex."

Thus it is evident that this plant of heavenly growth has struck root in the western quarter of the globe, and there, as well as here, will one day cover with its wide-spreading branches, and refresh with its life-giving fruit, innumerable multitudes of the ignorant poor; and the praises and thanksgivings of Sunday School scholars from each shore of the Atlantic mingling upon its waves shall swell above its thunders, and rise before the throne of the Eternal, a grateful memorial of the countries from which they ascend.

Only one more triumph of this mighty scheme remains to be recorded, but that is a splendid one, no less than its invasion of Asia, and its establishment amidst the temples and the gods of that part of the world which may be denominated the metropolis of idolatry. The first Sunday Schools in Asia were established by the Baptist missionaries at Serampore, but at what date does not appear. Their example was followed by their brethren the Wesleyan Missionaries in Ceylon, whose commencement of the good work is thus reported by Mr Harvard and Mr Clough, who were stationed in that island:

"June 4, 1815. We cannot conceal that the establishment of our Sunday School has given us favour in the eyes of many. It has certainly considerably tended to help on the subscription to our place of worship. We only consulted one friend, who stated insurmountable difficulties, and assured us that the time was not yet come, and that the people were not ripe for such an institution. However, we were determined, by the help of God, to make the trial; and now that we have upwards of two hundred and fifty children, and twenty teachers most cheerfully and freely engaged in instructing them every week, everyone is charmed, and several are surprised that so simple an idea did not occur to their minds before. We have the pleasure to inform you that, through the great kindness of the Hon. Robert Boyd, Member of Council, and Commissioner of Revenue, we have the use of the theatre for our Sunday School; and a better place could not have been chosen, it being so very central and commodious. We have quite a train of native children now in our school."

Thus a lodgement has been made by this institution in one of the outworks to the stronghold which Satan possesses in the eastern division of the earth. Other missionaries in India will soon follow the example thus nobly given, until successive triumphs of the cross over the powers of darkness shall open for this beneficent scheme an access to the territory of China; nor is the day perhaps so distant as despondency suggests, when it shall be announced in Britain that Sunday Schools are formed in the city of Peking. Hasten it, O Lord, in thine own time!

Thus widely and rapidly has this institution multiplied its funds, its objects, and its conquests to the present time. It is not possible even to hazard a conjecture as to the number of children and adults which are every Sabbath under the sound of Sunday School instruction throughout the world. Perhaps if I were to state them at a million I should not at all exceed the aggregate. What a reflection for the moralist and the Christian, the patriot and the philanthropist! What a wide and lovely scene for an enlightened and generous imagination to range over! A million scholars collected by myriads of teachers in mighty circles round the fountain of celestial truth, to cleanse the eyes of their understanding from the scales of ignorance and vice! Contracted must be the mind, and cold the heart, which can find nothing here to awaken its raptures. If there be a window in heaven from which the blessed inhabitants can look upon this lower world; or if a door be opened, through which the spirits of the just made perfect are ever permitted to visit the scenes of their terrestrial labours; O who can conceive the ecstasies with which the soul of Raikes must hover over the captivating scene! What a mighty reflux of delight must roll back from the tide of his benevolence, and reach him even upon the heavenly side of the shores of eternity! What accessions must be continually made to his bliss, while one and another soul is continually arriving in the realms of glory, to tell its inhabitants they were converted to God in a Sunday School! But here conjecture fails us.

If we turn from the past to the future our hopes leave even our success behind. But few years comparatively will pass before other writers will look back from a distance on progress of the Sunday School institution inconceivable to us, and sum up all that I have recorded, as but the very commencement of its operations, the first fruits of its victories, and as not worthy to extend beyond the first page of its history.

–1–

The Ultimate Object of Sunday School Instruction

IT is necessary to the success of any exertions whatever, that the object to which they are to be directed should be distinctly understood. Any confusion on this point will be attended with fluctuation of design and weakness of endeavour, but ill calculated to ensure success.

There is just ground to believe that many who are engaged in the work of Sunday School instruction, are but imperfectly acquainted with its ultimate end.

It is much to be feared as to some that in giving their assistance to this cause, nothing further enters into their view, *than communicating to the children an ability to read.* In the estimation of such people, the Sabbath institutions seem to rank no higher than ordinary day schools, where the offspring of the poor receive the elements of common education. Provided therefore they can assist their pupils to read with tolerable facility, they attain the highest object of their desires or expectations. How will such teachers be surprised when I inform them, that the top-stone of *their* hopes is but the foundation of their duties; and that the highest elevation of *their* purposes is but the beginning of the ascent which leads to the summit of the institution.

I admit that where no higher aim than *this* is taken, though very far below the proper mark, much benefit is likely to accrue to the children, to their immediate connections, and to society at large. Where no effort is made to form the character, and nothing more in fact is done than simply to communicate the art of reading, a vast advantage is conferred upon the children of the poor. It is the testimony of inspiration, "That for the soul to be without knowledge is not good;" and the whole history of man confirms the truth of the remark. The very first rudiments of knowledge, independently of any systematic attempt to improve the character, must have a moral tendency. In attaining the very lowest elements of education, the soul feels itself elevated, and, however it may be precipitated back again by the violence of its depravity, is conscious still that it has begun to ascend from the regions of sense. Ignorance debases and degrades the mind. It not only enslaves the intellect, but dims the eye by which the human conscience traces the natural distinction between right and wrong. "On the contrary," says Mr Hall, "knowledge expands the mind, exalts the faculties, refines the taste for pleasure, and, in relation to moral good, by multiplying the mental resources, has a tendency to elevate the character, and in some measure to correct and subdue the taste for gross sensuality." Hence it is obvious, that the very least and lowest end which, as Sunday School teachers, you can propose to yourselves in your labour has a tendency to benefit the interests of the poor. I wish, however, to remind you, that simply to teach the art of reading is the least and lowest end you can contemplate.

Others connect attention to *habits of order, industry and morality*, with the rudiments of knowledge, as the ultimate object of their efforts. They are most laudably anxious to form the character of the children, so as that they may rise into life an industrious, orderly, and sober race. This is of vast importance, and subordinate only to what I shall afterwards propose as the ultimate end of all your endeavours. Much of the peace, comfort, and safety of the community depends upon the character and habits of the poor.

If society be compared to the human frame, they are the feet and the hands: and how much do the ease and the welfare of the whole body depend upon the healthy state of the extremities! To tame the ferocity of their unsubdued passions; to repress the excessive rudeness of their manners; to chasten the disgusting obscenity of their language; to subdue the stubborn rebellion of their wills; to render them honest, obedient, courteous, industrious, submissive, and orderly, should be an object of great desire with all who are engaged in the work of Sunday School instruction. It should be your ceaseless effort to reform the vices, to heal the disorders, and exalt the whole character of the lower classes of society, by training up their offspring in "whatsoever things are true, whatsoever things are honest, whatsoever things are just, whatsoever things are pure, whatsoever things are lovely, whatsoever things are of good report." Then, to use the beautiful imagery of the prophet, "instead of the thorn shall come up the fir tree, and instead of the briar shall come up the myrtle tree."

Pleasing and important as such an object really is; delightful as it is to produce in the breast of a poor man a taste for reading, together with a habit of thinking and thus teach him to find entertainment at home, without being tempted to repair to the ale-house; delightful as it is to bring him into communion with the world of reason, and help him by the joys of intellect to soften the rigours of physical toil; delightful as it is to teach him to respect himself, and secure the respect of others, by industrious, frugal and peaceful habits: to assist him to become the instructor of his own domestic circle, and thus to raise him in their estimation; in short, delightful as it is to strip poverty of its most distressing appearances, and to remove its more painful privations of a temporal nature, this of itself, and alone, is far below the ultimate object of your exertions. You must look higher even than this for the summit of your hopes. A man may be all that I have represented; he may be industrious, orderly, moral, and useful in his habits, and still be destitute of that faith and "holiness, without which no man shall see the Lord."

Addressing you as believers in all that revelation teaches concerning the nature, condition and destiny of man, I must point your attention to an object which stands on higher ground than any we have yet contemplated. It is for you to consider, that each of the children who are every Sabbath beneath your care, carries in his bosom *a soul* as valuable and as durable as that which the Creator has lodged in your own. Neither poverty, ignorance, nor vice, can sever the tie which binds man to immortality. Every human body is the residence of an immortal spirit; and, however diminutive through childhood, mean from poverty, or filthy by neglect, the hovel may appear, a deathless being will be found within it. Every child that crosses the threshold of your school on Sunday brings to your care, and confides to your ability, *a soul*, compared with whose worth the sun is a bauble; and with whose existence time itself is but the twinkling of an eye.

And as those poor children partake with you in the dignity of immortality, so do they also *in the degradation and ruin of the fall.* The common taint of human depravity has polluted their hearts as well as yours. They, like you, in consequence of sin are under the curse, and stand exposed to everlasting misery. To them however the gracious scheme of redeeming mercy extends its blessings; and indeed by the express provisions of the Gospel charter, they are first among the objects to whom salvation is to be presented, "for the poor have the Gospel preached to them." Denied neither the privilege of immortality, nor the opportunity of eternal happiness, they are not exempt from the obligations of religion. Without the duties required in your own case, in order to eternal life, *they* will never possess it. Faith, repentance and holiness, regeneration, justification and sanctification, are as indispensable in *their* case as yours. Their danger of losing all the rich blessings of salvation, unless great exertions be made to instruct and interest their minds, is imminent and obvious. Dwelling in the walks of life where sin, in its most naked and polluting form, spreads destruction around; corrupted by their neighbours; nursed and nurtured in vice, in many cases, by the example of their parents; in manufacturing districts inhaling the moral contamination with which the atmosphere of almost every workshop is laden, how rapid is the growth of original corruption; how luxuriant the harvest of actual transgressions which spring from it; how little likely, without extraordinary efforts, are those unhappy youths to enter "the narrow path that leadeth to eternal life!"

Such are the children who flock every Sabbath to the schools where you are carrying on the business of instruction, and such their situation. Look round upon the crowd of *little immortals* by whom you are encircled every week; view them in the light which the rays of inspired truth diffuse over their circumstances; follow them in imagination, not only into the ranks of society, to act their humble part in the great drama of human life, but follow them down into that valley, gloomy with the shadows of death, from which they must come forth, those that have done well, to everlasting life, but those that have done ill, to everlasting shame and contempt: and while you see them plunging into the bottomless pit, or soaring to the celestial city, say what should be the ultimate object of a Sunday School teacher's exertions!

You are now quite prepared to assent to my opinion on this subject, when I thus state it. The ultimate object of a Sunday School teacher should be, in humble dependence upon divine grace, *to impart that religious knowledge, to produce those religious impressions, and to form those religious habits in the minds of the children, which will be crowned with the* SALVATION OF THEIR IMMORTAL SOULS; or, in other words, *to be instrumental in producing that conviction of sin, that repentance towards God, that faith in the Lord Jesus Christ, that habitual subjection in heart and life to the authority of the Scriptures, which constitute at once the form and power of* GENUINE GODLINESS.

Here then you see your object; and you perceive that it includes every other in itself. To aim at anything lower than this as your ultimate and largest purpose; to be content with only some general improvement of character, when you are encouraged to hope for an entire renovation of the heart, or merely with the formation of moral habits, when such as are truly pious may be expected; is to conduct the objects of your benevolence with decency down into the grave, without attempting to provide them with the means of a glorious resurrection out of it. To train them up in the way of sincere and undefiled religion is an object of such immense importance, that compared with it the ability to read and write, or even all the refinements of life, have not the weight of a feather in their destiny. And the truth must be told, that wherever religious education is neglected, the mere tendency of knowledge to the production of moral good is in most cases very lamentably and successfully counteracted by the dreadful power of human depravity.

Sunday Schools, to be contemplated in their true light, should be viewed as *nurseries for the church of God;* as bearing an intimate connection with the unseen world, and as ultimately intended to people the realms of glory with "the spirits of just men made perfect." To judge of their value by any lower estimate; to view them merely as adapted to the perishing interests of mortality, is to cast them into the balances of atheism, to weigh them upon the sepulchre and to pronounce upon their value without throwing eternity into the scale.

The salvation of the immortal soul, a phrase than which one more sublime or more worthy can never drop from the lips or the pen of man, describes your greatest and noblest purpose.

In what way this object is most likely to be effected, remains now to be considered.

1. Labour to impart to the children, as speedily as possible, a very *correct method of reading.*

This is the first thing to be attended to; and as it is the basis of all which is to follow, it should be done well. Considering an ability to read, as I do every other part of Sunday School tuition, as a means for the production of spiritual and moral good, I view it as of immense importance, that the children should be rendered as perfect as possible in this basic skill. Reading is a powerful auxiliary to the progress of piety and virtue, but it is attractive only when it is performed with facility; and therefore to allure the children to the pages of Revelation, or the perusal of good books, it is necessary to render their access as smooth as possible. If they often have to spell a word, and still more often to pass by a word which they cannot spell, they will either be much impeded in their instruction, or perhaps give up the matter in utter despair. Few have the courage, confidence and perseverance to pursue a course of self-tuition after they leave the school, if they do not acquire a tolerable facility in reading while they are there. It is of vast importance therefore that you should take peculiar pains in this preliminary step of the religious education of the children, in order that they may feel all that inducement to read which arises from the consciousness of being able to do it with ease and correctness. I am aware that admonition is exceedingly necessary on this head, and that many scholars quit our institutions most lamentably wanting in this the very ground work of instruction. It is a fact that many of those who apply for admission into our adult schools are young men and women who were but imperfectly taught when children in our Sunday Schools; and who could, therefore, have made but very little use of their Bible during those years when they had most leisure to read it.

2. You are to seek the great object of your labours by a course of religious instruction, *judiciously adapted to the capacity of the children.*

I take it for granted that the business of every school is so arranged as to allow to the teachers a sufficient opportunity for explaining and enforcing the principles of religion.

And here I think it right to remark, that, as the very first lesson of religious instruction, it is of vast importance to produce, even from its commencement, *a sort of trembling reverence for the authority of Revelation.* From the time a child is capable of receiving a sentiment on religion, he should be made to feel the obligation of the Word of God upon his understanding and conscience. The first idea which should be communicated to his mind, and which in every subsequent stage of education should be nursed and nurtured into a conviction inseparable from all his moral feelings, is that *the Bible is and must be true;* and that however singular, however beyond the range of our experience, or however miraculous any of its facts may be, and however incomprehensible are some of its doctrines, still they are all to be implicitly believed, because they are declared in the Word of God: so that one of the earliest and strongest associations of their minds shall be that formed between their idea of truth and everything contained in the holy Scriptures. From the beginning they should be instructed that all reasonings, views and feelings are to be brought into subjection to the inspired volume; and that from this authority in matters of religion there does and can lie no appeal. In order to this, the evidences of revealed truth should be laid before them in a familiar manner; and even before they are capable of estimating the weight of proofs, we should endeavour to produce a powerful conviction in them that the Bible is true. The reason for my insisting so much on this is a conviction that among the lower class of society there is a great deal of that low and ignorant scepticism which is produced in minds incapable of reasoning, by ridiculing facts which are beyond their experience, and truths which are above their comprehension. There is a sort of practical and vulgar infidelity which weaves its way into the dwellings of the poor, and they, in consequence of not being well-grounded in the persuasion that the Bible must be true whatever corrupt minds may say against it, often fall into its snares, and become its hapless victims.

What therefore I enjoin is to endeavour that the children's minds may be so rooted and grounded in the conviction of the truth of Revelation, that when a profane and artful opposer of the Scriptures shall attempt insidiously to shake their faith, by ridiculing any of the facts or sentiments of the sacred volume, they may shudder at the insinuation, and retire instinctively to the shelter of this immovable conviction, the Bible *must* be true.

Let it be an object of concern with you to impart to your pupils *a correct view of the leading truths of Revelation.* You know how to treat the opinion that the doctrines of the Gospel are quite unnecessary in the instruction of children, and that their attention should be exclusively confined to its moral precepts. Explain to them the moral attributes of the great God; his holiness, as opposed to all iniquity; his truth, as manifested in the giving of his Word; his mercy, which inclines him to pity the miserable. Teach them the purity of his law, as pronouncing condemnation on a sinful thought. Endeavour to make them understand the exceeding sinfulness of sin, as breaking through all the obligations imposed upon the conscience by the majesty and goodness of God. Strive to lead them to a knowledge of the total corruption of their nature, as the source and spring of their actual transgressions. Unfold to them their situation, as under the wrath of God, on account of their sins. Show them their inability either to atone for their guilt or renovate their nature. Lead them to Calvary, and explain the design of the Saviour's death as a sacrifice for sin, and teach them to rely upon his merits alone for salvation. Direct them to the Holy Spirit, as the fountain of grace and strength, for the renewal of their hearts. In connection with this, lay before them all the branches of Christian duty; those which relate to God, such as faith, repentance, love, obedience, and prayer; and those which relate to man, as obedience to parents, honesty to their employers, kindness to all. Enforce upon them the obligations of the Sabbath and public worship. Particularly impress upon them that genuine religion, while it is founded on a belief of God's Word, does not consist merely in abstract feelings or occasional duties, but in a principle of submission to the revealed will of Jehovah, implanted deep in the heart, pervading the conduct, and spreading over the whole character, so as to form a holy, moral, useful, happy man.

Such are the topics which you are to illustrate to the children; unquestionably the most important which can engage their attention. Much, however, depends upon the method you adopt for explaining them.

Of course you should allot a portion of time to the work of *catechising*. The experience of all ages bears testimony to the utility of this plan. If well improved it affords a most favourable opportunity for communicating religious knowledge. To accomplish this end it is necessary that you should do more than simply ask the questions, and receive the answers, as they are given in the book. To arrest and engage the minds of children, who consider it generally as nothing more than a school exercise, you must descend to familiar explanation. Every answer should be regarded as a text, which, by a few plain short remarks, you should illustrate to their understanding, and enforce upon their consciences. It will be found an excellent method to explain one Sabbath what is to be committed to memory during the week, and repeated as a task the next. As we always learn with greater ease and pleasure what we understand, this would facilitate the business of memory, and prepare them for the examination which should always take place when they are called upon to repeat the answers which had been previously explained to them.

It would greatly aid the business of religious instruction, if the children were encouraged to *commit to memory* hymns, and portions of the Word of God, especially the latter. The measure and the rhyme of poetry have attractions, which without great care on the part of the teacher are likely to induce a preference for hymns. The inspired volume should be elevated in their estimation above every other book. The very words, as well as sentiments, of Revelation, have a power and energy which the language of uninspired authors, however correct their opinions, does not possess. Divine truth, expressed in divinely inspired language, often strikes upon the conscience with a force which would be found in nothing else. As the children are likely to be influenced by other motives than a simple regard to their improvement, the discretion of the teachers should be employed in selecting passages of Scripture suitable to be learnt; especially remembering that, as whatever is committed to memory should be commended to the judgement, they should be more anxious for their pupils to learn *well* than learn *much*.

Select a passage, and assign it either to a whole class, or a part of it, to be learnt by the next Sabbath, when it will become the subject of examination; and in the meantime, consider what are the questions which it naturally suggests, that you may be prepared for the task. This is a most engaging and instructive method.

Another very judicious exercise for the children is to propose a question, and to require, by a certain time, passages of Scripture to prove and illustrate it; always taking care that the subjects of inquiry are plain, easy, and adapted to the capacity of the children.

Such exercises as these possess the happiest tendency. They are an admirable discipline for the intellectual powers, and train the mind to habits of reflection and diligent inquiry. They call the thinking principle into activity, and must produce considerable improvement in the mental character of the young. But these are the smallest advantages of the plan: it leads to an engaging and enlarged acquaintance with the Word of God, and establishes a sort of familiarity between the children and the Bible, as the man of their counsel, and the guide of their youth.

It would be well also occasionally to examine the children as to their remembrance of the texts and sermons which they hear in the house of God. This would keep their attention alive to what is delivered from the pulpit, and lead them to recognise their own interest in the solemnities of public worship.

Such, among other means of communicating religious instruction, appear to me to be eminently adapted to promote this important end.

3. But as very many know the theory of divine truth, without feeling its influence on the heart, or exhibiting it in the conduct; as they often see the right way without walking in it; and as it is only those who are renewed and sanctified by the truth who will be eternally saved, you must, to secure the ultimate object of your exertions, labour to produce *religious impression* as well as communicate religious instruction. I know it is God alone who can reach the heart; but he does it generally by pouring out his Spirit on judicious and well-adapted means. Direct then all your efforts to awaken the conscience, to interest the feelings, and to engage the whole soul in the pursuit of salvation and the business of religion. Let your aim be visible in your conduct, so that the children may be convinced that, until they are brought to fear God, and serve him in truth, you do not consider yourself to have attained the object of your labours. Let all you do be characterised by an impressive solemnity. Take care of treating sacred subjects with lightness. Never suffer the holy Scriptures to be read unless with the greatest reverence. Mingle a devotional spirit with all you do. Admonish and exhort the children with great seriousness, mixed with evident concern for their souls. Endeavour to awe them by the terrors of the Lord, and melt them by his mercies. Roll over them the thunders of Mount Sinai, and display to them the moving scenes of Mount Calvary. Remind them of their mortality, and bring before their imagination the scenery of the Day of Judgment. Seize every event that the dispensations of divine Providence may furnish to aid your endeavours. Relate to them instances of early piety, and at other times alarming cases of sudden dissolution. Watch for the appearance of religious concern, as that which can alone reward your labours, or satisfy your desires. Over every other kind of excellence than true religion, exclaim, "Ah! 'tis well, 'tis good, as far as it goes: but I want the fruits of immortality." When these begin to show themselves, hail the first buds of genuine religion with delight, shield them with a fostering care, and with a skilful hand direct their growth.

– 2 –

The Qualifications of
Sunday School Teachers

THIS is a part of the subject to which the attention of my readers should be directed with the deepest interest and most lively concern. The following enumeration will furnish rather an elevated standard: but instead of condemning it as too high, it should be your endeavour to see how near you can approach it.

1. It is exceedingly important that *you should be a partaker of real personal religion.*

By personal religion I mean more than a general profession of attachment to Christianity; more than a correct theory of religious sentiments; more than a stated attendance upon devotional forms; I mean *an experimental acquaintance* with the truths of the Gospel in their consoling and sanctifying influence. It is certainly very true that without such a state of heart you may be useful in promoting the subordinate ends of the institution, but you can scarcely be expected to reach the ultimate and supreme one. You may perform the humbler duties in this spiritual husbandry of gathering out the stones and preparing the soil, but to sow the seed of the kingdom must be left to other hands. You may, it is true, impart a knowledge of letters, and teach the children to read even the book of God; but to be the instrument of writing his laws upon their minds, and inscribing them upon their hearts, is an honour to which, without true piety, you cannot aspire. The teacher who is earnestly seeking the eternal salvation of the children occupies a station as far above *his* level who seeks nothing more than their temporal advantage, as the angel flying through the midst of heaven is above the traveller who is toiling across the low and sandy desert. If I were to delineate in picture the emblem of a Sunday School teacher's duty and employment, I would represent faith and love, like the two angels that conducted Lot from Sodom, leading between them a poor child to the cross, and while one was directing his eye to the means of salvation, the other should be pointing him to the realms of eternal glory. But will this apply to you without decided personal religion? O no. If you are unconcerned about your own soul; if you gaze with a tearless eye upon your own nature in ruins; how can it be expected you will mourn over the spiritual desolation you see in others? How can you teach an unknown God? How can you represent that Saviour as a pearl of great price who to you is a stone of stumbling? Can you illustrate in what manner the principles of divine truth should constrain the conscience and engage the affections; how they should become the elements of a new existence, and be breathed into the nostrils as the breath of spiritual life? What, this without experimental religion? The maxim, To teach you must *feel*, is most applicable to vital piety of all things. And as you will be without *ability*, so in the absence of this qualification you will be equally destitute of *inclination*, to seek the highest objects of your teaching. Can you feel really disposed to alarm, to stimulate, to admonish others, in reference to the salvation of their souls, when every word brings back upon yourself the keen reproach, "Physician, heal thyself"? A jealous conscience would not endure the insult; and to keep peace in your own bosom, you will inevitably keep from the children the care and benefits of which you have no personal experience. If he that winneth souls is wise, and you would start in this career of wisdom, and become candidates for this prize which excites the ambition of two contending worlds, first become wise unto salvation for yourselves, and then from the mighty impulse of that wisdom, seek the eternal welfare of the children.

2. A teacher should possess *an accurate and extensive acquaintance with divine truth.*

It is not possible, neither is it desirable, to ascertain the lowest measure of knowledge with which true godliness is compatible. In many cases the piety of the heart in reference to the ideas of the mind may be said to be the light shining in darkness. Far, very far removed from the *dawn* of divine truth in the soul, is the degree of knowledge which every teacher should seek to possess. Your views should be clear and extensive. To much love in the heart, you should seek to add much light in the mind. You should have such an acquaintance with your Bible, as to know to what parts of it more particularly to direct the attention of your scholars. You should have a competent knowledge of all its leading doctrines, and be able to cite with readiness particular passages to support them. Without this, how can you conduct the business of religious instruction with much effect? Remember, your class forms a kind of little planetary system, of which, so far as instrumentality is concerned, you are the central luminary. If conscious of any considerable defect in religious knowledge, let your office stimulate you to a more diligent perusal of the Word of God. With you it should be an object of great desire, not only to grow in grace, but also in the knowledge of God and our Saviour Jesus Christ. You should devote much time to reading the Scriptures and theological books.

3. *Gravity of deportment* is indispensably necessary.

Here I would not be understood as wishing to envelope the schools of religion in the gloom of melancholy and moroseness. You should be as remote from this disposition, as from its opposite extreme, trifling levity. A teacher of glad tidings should not array himself in sackcloth; nor should the messenger of mercy appear as sullen and repulsive as the spectre of the cloister.

Religion, when wrapped in gloom, will present but little that is attractive to children; nor will they be able to conjecture how a countenance that is professedly lifted up amidst the light of heaven, can present an aspect so threatening and so dark. Be it recollected however that the cheerfulness which true piety inspires, is holy and dignified like itself, and resembles, not the dissipating glare which is thrown over a city by the gaudy lights of an illumination, but that soft and soothing radiance which beautifies the face of nature on a summer's eve. Religion has its smiles; they are not borrowed, however, from the scenes of a ballroom, but from the splendid visions of eternity, and therefore, with the happiness of heaven, partake of something of its dignity. The topics of immortality sound badly from the lips of frivolity; and so uttered are sure to lose much of their effect.

The authority of a teacher, of whatever description may be his pupils, can be maintained only by *a dignified sedateness of manners.* If we may judge from the frequency with which it is enjoined in the New Testament, the Holy Spirit appears to attach great importance to this disposition; since not only are the office-bearers of the Christian church commanded to be grave, but even its ordinary members, and especially young men, are charged to show gravity and sincerity, as if it were hardly possible to be sincere in religion, without being serious in deportment.

If you see the importance of such a disposition, you will be impressed with the necessity of avoiding *a showy and expensive mode of dress.* These remarks apply, of course, more particularly to *female* teachers. A fondness for dress is one of the prevailing evils of the present day; and, unhappily, it has crept down into the lower classes of society, and imposes its tax upon those who are but ill able to support it. Of the multitude of unhappy females who have quitted the paths of virtue, the great majority have been first led astray by this vain and expensive propensity. The connection between wearing showy clothes, and delight in exhibiting them, is almost inevitable in ignorant and little minds; and this love of display has often first attracted and encouraged the eye of the seducer, just as brightly coloured feathers catch the attention of the hawk looking round for his prey. If one may judge from the conduct of the lower classes at the present time, they seem to be endeavouring to hide poverty beneath gaudy colours. Ten thousand evils will flow in upon society, (and they have already begun to flow), when the poor shall conclude that they are respectable in proportion as they are fine; and how much will this disposition be encouraged in the pupils, if it be enforced by the example of the teacher! The children must have far more dignity of mind, far more solid reflection, and far more just discrimination, than can be expected in their circumstances, not to be fascinated with an exhibition on your part of "broidered hair, or gold, or pearls, or costly apparel." To regard these things with indifference, when constantly displayed before their eyes, is too much to look for in them, when it is not found in you. With such objects before them, a whole train of the very worst feelings is likely to arise; admiration, envy, discontent, all are rapidly engendered. The rich velvet, and the glossy satin, together with feathers, flowers, and ribbons, have but little virtue to reconcile them to the coarser textures and the plainer hues of poverty.

Permit me then to recommend the utmost simplicity and neatness of apparel as of great importance in your office. Especially and earnestly do I enjoin the most scrupulous *modesty*. Even a distant approach to the indecency which has characterised some modern fashions would be offering poison to the morals of every child before whom it is displayed. I am not urging meanness, much less slovenliness or filthiness. These are a species of semi-vices wherever they exist; and are to be counteracted in young children by the instruction of your lips and the force of your example. What I recommend may be all summed up in two words, *modesty* and *neatness;* or, to express it in the language of an apostle, "Whose adorning, let it not be the outward adorning of plaiting the hair, and wearing of gold, or of putting on of apparel; but let it be the hidden man of the heart, in that which is not corruptible, even the ornament of a meek and quiet spirit, which in the sight of God is of great price."

4. A teacher should be intimately *acquainted with all the general proprieties of human conduct* which arise out of the distinctions of society and be deeply impressed with their importance.

You should not only clearly understand what is religiously and morally right, but also have a keen perception of those minor distinctions between right and wrong, which have been established by the authorised laws of human intercourse. You should be acquainted with the obligations of inferiors to superiors; and of persons in dependent stations of life to those who are their supporters or employers. You should be alive to all the little niceties of behaviour demanded by courtesy, and be able to expose to the children the impropriety of any instance of rudeness, incivility, or ingratitude. Christianity, instead of sinking the distinctions of society, has elevated and guarded them; and indeed has employed its most sublime and powerful motives to enforce the minutest duties of social life. The children of the poor, especially in large manufacturing towns, are often exceedingly destitute of that respectful deportment towards their superiors which the order of society necessarily requires. This defect it is your duty as much as possible to supply. A civil, submissive, respectful habit is not to be considered as merely constituting the polish of *general* character, but in some measure preparing for religious impression. A rude, uncivil, intractable youth is the last in the school in whose heart holy emotions are likely to be produced. He who feels little respect for human authority is ill-prepared for bowing with humility before that which is divine.

5. It is very necessary that "an instructor of babes" should be able to *communicate knowledge in a simple and familiar manner.*

This is a talent peculiarly requisite in those who are entrusted with the education of children. The mere *possession* of knowledge does not qualify for the business of instruction, except it be attended with *an aptitude in communicating it.* Every judicious teacher will consider the character of his audience, and adapt his communications to their capacity. If what he says is not understood, he may as well talk in a foreign language. Children require a very different mode of instruction from what may be adopted in the case of well-educated adults. They are ignorant of the first principles of divine truth. Nothing must be taken for granted in teaching them. You must assume nothing; everything is to be communicated. Perhaps it is the fault of all teachers, not excepting those who deliver their instructions from the pulpit, that they proceed on the supposition that their audience have more knowledge than they really possess. They take far too much for granted. This must be particularly avoided with children in Sunday School. Of by far the greater number of them it may be affirmed, that they have not a single idea on the subject of religion, but what they will derive from you; and you are to be very careful in presuming upon what they have derived from you.

The same remarks will apply to language as to sentiments. Their knowledge of words is as contracted as their range of ideas; and in order really to instruct them, you must always remember the extent of their vocabulary. Your message cannot be too simple and familiar, provided it be not vulgar.

> "Nothing," says Mr Cecil, "is easier than to talk to children; but to talk to them as they ought to be talked to, is the very last effort of ability. A man must have a vigorous imagination, and be able to call in illustrations from the four corners of the earth; for he will make little progress but by illustration. It requires great genius to throw the mind into the habit of children's minds. I am surprised at nothing which Dr Watts did, but his *Hymns for Children*. Other men could have written as well as he, in his other works; but how he wrote those hymns I know not."

An *aptitude* to teach children then in their own way, while it is necessary as a qualification, should be sought as an acquirement. I know of no better method by which this talent may be attained than to read with attention the most approved works which have been written for children, in order to mark and imitate the style there adopted. Such, for instance, are Dr Watts' *Divine Songs for Children*, and Miss Taylor's *Hymns for Infant Minds*, together with any other books which possess simplicity without meanness. If those who wish to cultivate an elegant style read the standard works of the language, surely they whose office requires simplicity of address should take the same means to excel in their appropriate attainment.

6. *A heart most deeply interested in the work* is a very necessary qualification.

This is a cause which leaves no room for the operation of those principles to which, in the general concerns of mankind, so large a portion of human activity may be traced. Here, neither avarice, nor ambition, nor vanity, can have any place, or contribute in the least degree towards success. Without a heart deeply interested in the work, there can be no energy and no success. That teacher who feels no conviction of the importance of the cause, and no concern about its issue; who has been brought into the school by no motive at all, – or, at best, no other motive than to follow the example, or gratify the desires, of others; – has entered upon a station for which he is ill-qualified, and from which the sooner he retires the better. Without a most benevolent attachment to the duties of your office, you cannot perform them with much effect. This alone will carry you through the difficulties, discouragements, and sacrifices which it calls you to sustain. Without such an anxious desire to be successful as shall constrain you to that activity which is requisite to ensure success, you will do but little. It is painful to observe with what sauntering indifference some young people perform the duties of the school. They begin with weariness, and end with disgust. It is very evident that, whatever else they devote to the cause, they have never given their hearts.

7. *A patient temper* is exceedingly requisite.

The business of instruction, especially the instruction of poor children, who have everything to learn, will often require the very utmost stretch of forbearance. You will meet with so much constitutional dullness, so much heedless attention, so much wilful neglect, and so much insolent disobedience, that, unless your feelings are under considerable control, you will often be hurried into excesses of impatience, disgraceful to yourself and injurious to your pupils. The little vexations and irritations which arise to try a Sunday School teacher's temper are innumerable and unceasing. Yet, to be successful, you must be patient. You must discipline your temper until it is quite under restraint. A peevish or passionate manner, excited by every little irritating circumstance, renders you exceedingly unfit to deal with the untutored minds and habits of the children of the poor. In many cases impatience in the teacher must be exceedingly injurious to the improvement of the scholar. Some minds are very slow in their advances, very timid in their steps, and require the most affectionate forbearance to be kept from utter despair, and to be encouraged to go on at all: and harsh impetuosity would at once overwhelm them with confusion and dismay. Very, very often is a pupil thrown into such inextricable disorder by a hasty and terrifying sally of the master's impatience, that memory and judgement both forsake him in his fright, and leave him the motionless victim of injudicious anger. A person that does not have the patience to communicate knowledge drop by drop, should never think of undertaking the instruction of ignorant children, since it is utterly impossible to pour it into their minds by copious streams. We have not forgotten how slow and unwilling we were to receive the elements of education; but as all children are very much alike in this respect, we may take our own experience with respect to others as a tolerably correct measure of the pains which were taken with ourselves, and find in this no weak motive to seek the qualification which I now commend.

– 3 –

Directions as to the Duty
of a Teacher

HAVING disclosed to you the ultimate object of your exertions, and prescribed the qualifications necessary for accomplishing it, I shall now lay down some directions for the regulation of your conduct.

1. There should be a *discriminating attention to the different capacities and tempers of the children.*

A Sunday School may be considered as a plantation of young minds, the trees of which strike root in different manners, and blossom at various times; each requiring a method of culture adapted to its nature. Some need to be brought into the sun, others to be kept in the shade. Some need to have their growth repressed; others to have it stimulated. Children vary exceedingly in their capacities for learning. Perception is more quick, memory more retentive, comprehension more enlarged in some than in others. What is industry in one is indolence in another. Of this the teacher should be aware, lest, by expecting the same in both cases, he produce despondency in the former, or encourage idleness in the latter. Nothing is more discouraging throughout the whole range of education than to have the mind put upon exertions to which its faculties are unequal. The spirit in such a case, like a camel that has sunk beneath his burden, lies down in despair with scarcely a struggle to rise. It is of immense importance that you should know the real capacity of your children, and that you should never require of them impossibilities. You will often need much penetration to discriminate between a want of inclination and a want of ability; this, however, may be acquired.

The *temper* as well as the *mind* will require the same judicious attention. Some are timid, and will need great pains to produce in them more confidence in themselves; others are forward, and must be assiduously taught to be more diffident. Some are open and sincere; others are artful and designing. Sometimes you will find a character of such tenderness, that harshness would be like supporting a child's head by a strap of iron; and then again you will meet with such hard, incorrigible stubbornness, that lenient softness would be like tying down the branches of the mountain oak with a silken thread. Study then the character of the children. Minds, like locks, have different and often difficult wards; the same key will not open them all, yet all may be opened by a skilful locksmith.

It is astonishing what may be effected in the work of education by a little *ingenuity and invention*. There are some teachers who are like quack physicians, having an elixir which they administer in every case. They never vary the application. A command, a threat, and a blow; and if this does not succeed, the case is abandoned as desperate; whereas a little variation in the mode of treatment would have carried the point, and ensured success. We want more *science* in the business of education. To a certain extent you should be experimentalists upon the human mind; and when you meet with a case which ordinary methods do not reach, you should call to your assistance the powers of invention, and try the effect of new measures. I will here insert two anecdotes illustrative of my meaning. Mr Raikes was in the habit of visiting the parents and children belonging to his schools at their own houses. He called on a poor woman one day, and found a very refractory girl crying and sulking. Her mother complained that correction was of no avail, and that an inflexible obstinacy marked her conduct. After asking the parent's leave, he began to talk seriously to the girl; and concluded by telling her, that, as the first step towards amendment, she must kneel down and ask her mother's pardon. The girl continued sulky. "Well then," said he, "if you have no regard for yourself, I have much regard for you. You will be ruined and lost, if you do not begin to be a good girl; and if you will not humble yourself, I must humble myself, and make a beginning for you." With that he knelt down on the ground before the child's mother, and put his hands together, with all the ceremony of a juvenile offender, and supplicated pardon for the guilty daughter. No sooner did the stubborn girl see him on his knees on her account, than her pride was overcome at once, and tenderness followed; she burst into tears, and throwing herself on her knees, entreated forgiveness; and, what was still more pleasing, she gave no trouble afterwards.

What would many people have done in this instance? Uttered a scolding threat, and left the girl the miserable victim of her own bad temper. A little science, or, in other words, a little ingenuity, effected a reformation, for which perhaps that child blesses the name of Raikes to the present hour.

Mr Lancaster had once under his care a boy of the most indolent and intractable habits, on whom the ordinary methods of punishment produced no effect. He resolved, as the case seemed almost desperate, to try an experiment. He placed him as monitor over an inferior class; and, in order more effectually to awaken a feeling of interest and excite a habit of application, he opposed his class to another in a contest to come off at a week's end, proposing a reward to that monitor whose class was victorious. The experiment succeeded to admiration. Emulation was excited in the boy's mind. During the probationary week he was every morning at school in good time, urging on his class to the most vigorous exertions. His truant habits were now broken; and, rewarded by success, he became from that time a pattern of application.

By teachers less versed in the art of instruction, this boy would have been given up as incorrigible. You perceive what I mean by science and invention in education. Cultivate it. Indolence may sometimes be excited, where it cannot be driven. And one vice where it cannot be forcibly and immediately eradicated, may be starved and withered in the shadow of some opposite virtue, which a skilful and assiduous hand may raise against it.

2. *Exercise great judgment in the application of rewards and punishments.*

I am not now going to propose any particular kind of rewards and punishments; as this little volume is not intended to regulate the formation of schools, but is addressed to teachers individually, who are already engaged in supporting the order and arrangements of the school to which they belong. My remarks will therefore apply to the subject generally.

The proper application of rewards and punishments is the most difficult part of the business of instruction. To perceive the first buddings either of excellence or of vice, when the former needs most to be encouraged, and the latter may be most easily destroyed, requires a most watchful and discriminating eye. To cherish merit by reward, and at the same time not to promote the growth of pride and selfishness, which are so apt to spring up by its side in the forcing heat of excessive commendation, requires uncommon skill; and no less judgement is necessary in the case of punishment, lest by pulling up some noxious weed with too violent a hand, we tear up with it some better plant.

With respect to *reward*, I advise that, as much as possible, you make a child's own feelings his reward. External stimulants, I am aware, are sometimes necessary. Indolence must often be roused by the proposal of a prize, the value of which ignorance can comprehend, and be excited to desire. Anything is an advantage which moves the stagnant dullness of a mind after the failure of every other plan. But, as a system, I recommend you, as much as possible, to make your children a reward to themselves. By a little pains you may make them conscious of the pleasure of good behaviour, and the advantage of knowledge. When they have succeeded in a lesson, or an effort at good conduct, send them to their own bosom for a rewarding smile, and endeavour to make them aware of the value of that reward. By this means you elevate the tribunal and strengthen the authority, of conscience. This powerful principle is often totally neglected in the business of instruction. Its dictates are scarcely ever enforced, its authority seldom exhibited, and its solemn awards entirely super-seded by a bribing, hireling system of mercenary rewards. In the education of the heart, conscience is the great auxiliary, whose aid should be perpetually engaged. When a child has behaved so as to deserve commendation, instead of being judiciously instructed by his teacher in the pleasure of doing right, I acknowledge it is a much more easy method of reward to confer a ticket, which at some future day, is to be transmuted into money; but it is more than question-able whether it is the most effectual method. I repeat, I am not for excluding all external rewards; but I urge as pre-eminently important an endeavour to produce, in the minds of the children, a conviction that one of the best rewards for doing right is the pleasure of doing it.

Much the same strain of remark will apply to *punishment*. Chastisement is sometimes necessary. Even corporeal punishment, although it should be excluded as a system, may perhaps, in some cases of extremity, be resorted to, with success, like violent medi-cines. In all cases of chastisement, a teacher should carefully ascer-tain the degree of crime, and never forget to discriminate between sins of inadvertence and wilful depravity. Between the thoughtless follies of childhood, and those actions which are deeply dyed with criminality there is a wide difference, of which you should never lose sight. The teacher who, in the infliction of punishment, removes all the distinctions which exist between different classes of offence, is in the fair way of effacing from the minds of his children the natural distinction between right and wrong. *Endeavour to keep your own temper*. Never is a cool, dispassionate manner more necessary than when administering reproof, or inflicting punishment. Grinding teeth, flashing eyes, quivering lips, or angry words, are very unlikely means to bring a child to penitence. They may terrify, but will not melt. They may extort confession, but will not produce conviction. Enveloped in the mist of passion, how can you discriminate the precise degree of punishment requisite to produce repentance! *Let chastisement always be attended with an obvious regard to the interests of its subject*. No censor is so awful, or so effectual, as love; and no reproofs sink so deeply in the heart, as those which fall from the lips of affection. Mercy would soften the mind for the impres-sions of justice. Where there is a conviction that you chastise for the children's benefit, and not to gratify your own feelings, sub-mission, if not reformation, will generally follow. *Your great object in every case of misconduct should be to produce a cordial concern for the fault.* This is the very end of punishment. Without a perception of the impropriety of his conduct, and real sorrow for his offence, whatever punishment a child may receive, no solid basis is laid for reformation; and therefore very little is effected. By calm statement, by mild and forcible expostulation, by an appeal to the understand-ing and feelings of children, much, except in cases of incorrigible obduracy, may be effected in leading to genuine penitence. Great pains should be taken in every instance of moral delinquency to convince them that *their offence is committed chiefly against God*, and not merely in opposition either to the rules of the school, or the will of the teacher. It should be represented as a sin to be confessed to God, and for which there is no pardon but through the blood of the Saviour. Great judgement should be exercised in endeavouring to conduct the whole business of punishment in such a manner as shall be least likely to irritate or exasperate the feelings of the delinquent. Surgeons, when it is necessary to employ the knife, are very careful to keep the whole frame as cool as possible, and to choose a time for operation when the diseased part is least under the power of inflammation. Select *your* times; and particularly remember not to push the rigours of punishment too far, nor continue them too long. The moment you perceive that the mind is softened to real concern for the fault, and that stubbornness or impenitence has given way to docility or contrition, it is time for punishment to cease. Beyond this it would be breaking the bruised reed, and nipping the buds of reformation by the chilling influence of despair. In short, as in the business of reward, so also in its opposite, make great use of the children's own feelings. Put the rod into the hand of conscience, and excite a trembling dread of the strokes which are inflicted by this internal censor.

3. Discharge the duties of your office in a conciliating and *affec-tionate manner*.

God, who framed the constitution of the human mind, and con-structed all its mechanism, has Himself informed us what are the springs of action which should be chiefly touched by those who have anything to do in guiding its operations. "I drew them, saith Jehovah," speaking of His conduct towards the Israelites, "with the cords of love, and the bands of a man." Here, in this single short expression, we have compendiously expressed the whole theory of human government, whether it apply to families, schools, or nations; whether it be designed to control the savage or the sage. This verse, which contains the philosophy of government, should be studied by everyone who has anything to do with his fellow-men in the way of enlightening their minds, improving their hearts, forming their manners, or exacting their obedience. "The *cords of love* are the *bands of a man.*" In prescribing to you therefore the manner in which your duties are to be discharged, I must enjoin an affectionate and conciliating temper. But I would not be understood as here promoting that weak and foolish indulgence, which drops the reins of authority, and, by abandoning the children to their own inclinations, is still more destructive than the sternest tyranny. The temper that I mean is perfectly compatible with the most inflexible authority, but it expresses itself in *tender* and *gentle* language. The law of kindness is on its lips. Its commands and prohibitions are firm but mild. It avoids a surly, stern, repulsive tone; and often distributes to its objects looks and smiles which enter into their very hearts, and win them as captives to itself. It represses all that impatience which the ignorance, follies, and vices of the children, without great watchfulness, have a tendency to produce; and renders its possessor long-suffering and condescending. A teacher, adopting such a method, takes the nearest road to the hearts of the youths committed to his care. He will secure their affection, and thus hold in his hand the key of their disposition. You mistake, greatly mistake, if you suppose a stern, tyrannical manner is necessary to maintain your authority. Besides, it becomes you to recollect, that you are not mere ordinary schoolmasters: you are teachers of *religion*, and of that religion which has so much to do with love. It is the duty of your office to teach the children the knowledge of that great Being, of whom it is said, "GOD IS LOVE;" to point to the cross of Jesus, and instruct them in the height, and breadth, and length, and depth of the love of Christ, which passes knowledge; to repeat to them severally the commands of the two tables, and inform them that love is the fulfilling of the whole law; to implant in them the three cardinal virtues of Christianity, faith, hope, love, and to inform them that the greatest of them is love; in short, to teach them that godliness, the essence of which in this world, and its perfection in the world to come, is LOVE. How ill-adapted, how inconsistent, how derogatory to such an office, is a harsh, surly, and tyrannical method of expression! In teaching the religion of Jesus, we must exhibit his spirit, as well as teach his doctrines; we must copy him who as a teacher was meek and lowly in heart: for it should never be forgotten that in his religion, mercy and truth meet together.

4. With an affectionate unite *a dignified manner.*

I have already hinted that the two qualities are by no means incompatible with each other. Their union forms the very perfection of official conduct. Condescension is not necessarily connected with degradation; nor is it requisite to be familiar in order to be affable. Remember you are placed on an eminence above your children, and, however affection may lead you to *stoop* from it with kindness, in order the more effectually to reach them, still you must never *descend* from it so as to be upon their level. Between you and them there is a boundary line which must be mutually observed; and, in order to keep them from overstepping it on their side, do not approach too near it on your own. You *must* keep up your authority; for if you cannot ensure obedience you had better retire. Let your method of addressing them in common conversation be dignified and respect-ful. Call them by their proper names, and never apply the abbrevi-ated terms of vulgar phraseology. Avoid all jesting and low familiar-ity, together with the broad laugh of jocular merriment.

If you would have them respect your authority never trifle with it yourself. Let them see that you govern from principle, and not from caprice. In order to this, never require anything but what is rea-sonable, and insist upon the performance of all you require. Always deliberate before you command or threaten, and then never relax afterwards. Your great aim should be that they may both love and respect you.

5. *Pursue your exertions with unwearied perseverance.*

It was little to the honour of Reuben when his dying father thus delineated his character, "Unstable as water, thou shalt not excel." Instability is a great blemish of character: occasional excellence may conceal it for a season, but does not remove it. It is in general contemptible; but when it affects other people, it is cruel. Like the fig tree which the Saviour blasted, it excites our hopes only to disappoint them. There are some people whose activity for *a season* is prodigious. For a while they are all bustle and energy, but it is only for a while. I will not say that their exertions are utterly useless. Their zeal serves the part of thunderstorms in the atmosphere of benevolence; its roll is impressive, and its flashes as vivid as lightning, but they are also just as transient. Still, even the storm is useful, though in a degree very inferior to influences more steady, permanent and genial. How often have we had to lament the sudden resignation of teachers, whose labours required nothing but continuance to render them incalculably useful; but over whom we have exclaimed with a sigh, "Ye did run well: what hath hindered you?"

It will be proper to enumerate here some of the causes which frequently operate in producing a lack of the virtue I am now urging.

In some cases a lack of perseverance arises from *the self-denying nature of the employment, the difficulties and sacrifices of which were not previously considered.* In prospect of any intended labour, it is the part of wisdom to sit down and count the cost. Where this is neglected, even the smallest difficulties, as they come upon us when neither expecting them, nor prepared for them, are likely to have a very discouraging effect on the mind. It is vain to deny, and useless to conceal, that the office of a Sunday School teacher is attended with no trifling sacrifices of ease and comfort, which, unless they are foreseen, will in all probability soon drive them from the work. Should these pages meet the eye of anyone who is about ignominiously to retire from it, on finding that he has to undergo more trials than he expected, I entreat him to consider the importance of the cause which he is disposed to abandon. Let him meditate upon the worth of souls, and consider the children's interests for two worlds, which depend so much upon religious instruction; and then say if he ought not to blush at the thought of retreating.

Did the Son of God labour through a life of poverty, and agonise in a death of torture for immortal souls; and will you cast from you all care for their interests because a little sacrifice of time and ease is required on the Sabbath? Can you pretend to fellowship with Christ? If selfishness has not chilled your blood at its fountain, let it rise into your cheek as the blush of holy shame, and be the signal from this hour for rallying your retreating benevolence.

Some teachers have been induced to give up their employment *on account of a misunderstanding with their associates*. It is much to the reproach of human nature, that there is no object, however remote from the usual track of discord, however elevated above the mists of passion, or however removed from the common objects of selfishness, but it sometimes becomes the occasion of strife and alienation among those who support it. One should imagine, if experience were not a more credible witness than imagination, that the regions of benevolence were too rarefied an atmosphere for discord to breathe in. But we know to the contrary. Offences among the active supporters of a Sunday School are, alas, too common, and have driven many a valuable teacher away from his office. Let those who are under the influence of such a temptation, and have well-nigh resolved to quit their posts because of some injury which they have received, seriously consider what the poor children have done that *they* are to be objects of their revenge; for on them at last the anger falls. Let such teachers imagine the great God following them into their retirement, and proposing to them a question similar to that with which he surprised his disheartened prophet: "What doest thou here Elijah?" Would they venture to reply, or if they did, would it not be with trembling and confusion, "Lord, I was offended by my fellow-teachers, therefore I determined to give up my employment altogether!" "And what," it may be expected would Jehovah reply, "have those poor, ignorant, and, in this case, innocent children done, that they must suffer for the wrong thou hast received? Have I borne with thy offences and provocations, lo these many years, and never forsaken thee: and yet now for one slight injury dost thou forsake both my cause, and the interests of those poor babes that I had entrusted to thy care? Is this thy gratitude; thy obedience; thy religion?" Bow to the rebuke. Confess your folly. Be reconciled to the offender: and *persevere* in your duty.

Closely connected with this is *a dislike to some of the arrangements of the school, which not infrequently induces a teacher to make their alteration a condition of his continuing in office.* Such a concession cannot and ought not to be made unless the managers are convinced that the proposed alterations are for the benefit of the institution; and even then they ought not to be made with the view of gratifying an individual, but of improving the school. The disposition which leads a man to say, "Unless you alter this or that, I will immediately resign," with whatever plausible excuses it may be covered, is in reality nothing more or better than arrogance. Such teachers would do well to consider what would be the consequence if *everyone* had like themselves an alteration to propose as a condition of their continuance. They can scarcely pretend to be actuated by feelings of benevolence; since, whatever defects or imperfections they may discover in the school, they can certainly do much more good by continuing than by retiring. If they are really convinced that the system of instruction would be improved by the adoption of their views, and are conscious of being actuated by benevolence and not merely by self-will, then, in the spirit of a true reformer, they should continue in their office with the hope of one day being able to accomplish the object of desire.

In some cases young people have quitted their office *because there were none in the school of equal standing with themselves in life.* What! shall pride, that disgusting and destructive vice, be allowed admission to the field of mercy's sacred labours? What! must our very compassion be made dependent on the finery which the milliner, the jeweller, or the tailor can supply? That the frivolous and the worldly should refuse to resort to a place where correspondent glitter is not to be found is not surprising; but to refuse to distribute the benefits of instruction to the ignorant, and the blessings of salvation to the perishing, unless we have by our side one as well dressed as ourselves, seems the very climax of all that is absurd in human pride. Is this then a cause which can be ennobled by the splendour, or degraded by the obscurity, of its active supporters? Is it not enough that you are employed as the dispensers of God's richest gifts, and engaged for the benefit of immortal interests? The loftiest seraph that glows and burns in the temple above would, if so commissioned by his God, accept with gratitude the office you are disposed to vacate, and would think himself most honourably employed in teaching the knowledge of his exalted Lord, though his pupils were the poorest of children, and his associates the poorest of teachers. If, however, you must have fellow-workers who are your equals or superiors, you have only to look up with the eye of faith, and you would find yourself surrounded by ministers and missionaries, prophets and apostles, the wise and good of every age; who have all been pursuing, though in another way, the same grand object that you are seeking. And what is even this to the thought of being, although in the humblest sense, a fellow-worker with God and Christ in the redemption of a lost and miserable world?

Marriage has very frequently put an untimely close to a teacher's labours. I have seen very many instances in which the next Sabbath after the conjugal union has been formed, both parties have relinquished their office at the school. Does that union then, which was designed by its divine Author as the basis of society, release us from a single obligation to promote its welfare? Or do we acquire a sanctity of character by becoming married which is profaned by exposing it in a Sunday School? Or do the tender affections which this connection produces unfit the parties for an office one qualification of which is love? I acknowledge that in many, perhaps in most cases, the withdrawing of *females* becomes a matter of necessity when they give birth; but for a young *man* to give up his attention to the cause of God, the very first Sabbath after he has received the greatest relative blessing heaven has to bestow, is a cold expression of gratitude to his Benefactor. Until a rising family of his own prefer more just and sacred claims upon his time than the children of the poor it is both absurd and cruel to take it away from them. How can he better prepare himself to become the preceptor of the little circle that may one day surround his own fireside than by acquiring the art of instruction among the sons and daughters of strangers?

Such are the more prevailing causes that produce a want of perseverance, and such the manner in which they may be removed.

6. I mention *constancy* as exceedingly important in the manner of discharging the duties of a teacher's office.

This perhaps may seem like a repetition of the last direction; but the qualities recommended differ. By perseverance I intend *a continuance in office;* and by constancy a *steady, uniform, and undiverted discharge of its duties.* In most large towns circumstances are continually occurring which put this virtue to the test. Some popular minister is to preach; or one of the resident ministers is to preach a charity sermon, or funeral discourse: on such occasions, without a firm and steady attachment to the business he has undertaken, a teacher is in great danger of being induced to quit his post.

There is one sect in the religious world, which, although not enumerated in any book of denominations, or in any theological dictionary; and although it has neither distinct creed, nor separate temples, still is entitled to a specific notification: this sect I shall denominate the *Curiosi;* their identifying trait is *a love of novelty.* They belong to any preacher who for the time can interest them by something new; and they attach themselves to every congregation that has something going on out of the common way. Thus, as they are carried along the stream of profession, they are like twigs and chips floating down near the bank of a river, intercepted by every weed, and whirled in every little eddy.

If you would be a useful or respectable teacher, you must not belong to this denomination. It does not rank very high in heaven above, or earth beneath. They would gladly persuade you that, like the bee, they are sucking honey from every flower; but more like the butterfly, they rove through all the garden of the Lord, not to sip the most luxurious, but to flutter with a vain and useless volatility round the most gaudy blossoms within the sacred enclosure. Be always at your post; and let it be your glory to find what powerful attractions you can resist, rather than be absent from your needy charge.

7. *Punctuality* in a teacher is vitally connected with the prosperity of the school.

When one considers the importance of the object in which you are engaged, and adds to this the little time which at most you can command for seeking it, one might have presumed that it would be quite unnecessary to caution you against making that little less. And yet it is painful to be obliged to assert that there is scarcely one evil, under which the whole system more severely suffers, than *a want of punctuality* in the teachers. It is an evil which eats into the very core of the institution. Precisely in the degree in which it exists, the order of the school must be interrupted, the solemnity of instruction be disturbed, and the whole machine be impeded. Nor will the mischief stop here. The children, perceiving that it is useless to be there before their teachers, and imitating their irregularity, will sink into the same habits of inattention and neglect. Late masters must make late scholars. It is useless for you to admonish your class to be early, if by example you instruct them to be late.

There are a variety of causes which lead to the evil of which I now complain.

A thoughtless disregard to the importance of punctuality in general is observable in some people. They are always and in everything behind-hand. If they have an engagement, they never think of preparing for it until the time for it is past. On the Sabbath they do not set off to public worship until the clock reminds them they ought at that moment to be in their pew. "A few minutes," they lazily exclaim, "can make no great difference." A few minutes make no difference! If everyone in everything were to act upon this principle but for one day, the world would be in chaos. This procrastinating temper is a bane under the influence of which the interests of society are suffering in a thousand ways; and that man would deserve the thanks of his species, who could furnish the most effectual antidote against it. *There is a time for everything: and let everything be done in its time.* In common language we speak of making up for lost time, but this is impossible. A moment lost can never be recovered.

Late rising on Sunday morning is a great obstacle in the way of punctuality. Perhaps I shall be thought uncharitable in expressing my fear that many professing Christians protract their slumbers to an unusual length on the morning of Sundays; and thus convert that day, which was mercifully intended as a season of rest, into a period of indolence. Considering how closely the world and its concerns follow us on other days, one might imagine that we should feel disposed to make the Sabbath as long as possible. It is the last day we ought to shorten; and were our souls in a state of high spiritual prosperity, we should, like the lark, be soaring towards heaven upon the wings of the morning, while the greater part of the world below us was still wrapped in silence and in sleep, and, like the nightingale, continue to pour forth our songs in the night, when the multitude around us, to relieve the tedium of the sacred day, had prematurely gone to rest. But consider, *your* sloth defrauds not only your own souls, but also the souls of your children at the school. The dreams of such forbidden slumber, to be characteristic, should present you with a shepherd depriving his lambs of their food. Rising late, you are often driven to the school without prayer and without preparation, and even then are often long after the time. Every beam of the morning, as it gently touches the lids of your eyes, seems to address you in the language of Christ to His slumbering disciples: "Why sleep ye? Rise, and pray." Or, if this be too gentle a voice to rouse you from your slumbers, let harsher tones disturb you: "What meanest thou, O sleeper? Arise, call upon thy God."

Another cause of late attendance is *too much time employed at the dinner table*. Are there Christians who devote the Sabbath to more than ordinary gratification of the palate, and who, in order to provide for their pleasure, employ their servants or themselves during the most precious portion of the day in preparing for their table? Alas, to the shame of many who make large professions, this question must be answered in the affirmative. In some cases it is beyond a teacher's control to alter the arrangements of a family; but it is within everyone's ability to content himself with anything the house affords, rather than be late at school, through waiting for the joint still at the fire. Do I ask a costly sacrifice for the interests of the children? What! *a warm dinner* on Sundays too much to give up for those souls for which the Saviour gave His *blood?* this too much to relinquish, in order that you may hasten with the bread of life to those who are perishing for lack of it? Can you grudge *this* gratification, when it is to enlarge your opportunity of endeavouring to save those souls, which if finally lost, shall never have the temporary mitigation of their torments, that even a drop of water affords to a burning tongue?

Let me urge with peculiar earnestness, a strict regard to *punctuality*. That you may feel more strongly the obligations to this. I again entreat you to recollect for how short a space of time the children can enjoy your instructions. A few hours on the Sabbath, with respect to most of them, is all the time through the whole week during which they hear or see anything like religion. Make not that little less.

8. Crown all your labours with *fervent and habitual prayer.*

It is important for you, in all your exertions, to bear in mind the total and universal depravity of the human race.

By total depravity, I do not mean that men or children are as bad as they can be; for in general they lie under strong restraints. Not that they are all equally wicked; for some are more restrained than others. Not that they are destitute of everything useful and lovely in society; their social affections are often strong and praiseworthy. Not that the *form* of their actions is always wrong; the contrary is manifestly true. What I mean by total depravity, is an entire destitution in the human heart by nature of all spiritual affection and holy propensities.

In this view every child that comes to your school is, until renewed by divine grace, totally depraved. To change this state of the mind, and produce a holy bias; to create a new disposition; to turn all the affections into a new channel, and cause them to flow towards God and heaven, is the work of the omnipotent and eternal Spirit, but he, in the execution of his purposes, generally employs the instrumentality of man. Now this view of the case must be ever before your mind; it must mingle with all your plans, and direct all your exertions. You must accurately understand the nature of the materials on which you have to work, and be intimately acquainted with the source from which success is to be expected. You must sow the seed in due season with the diligence of the husbandman, and then exercise like him an unlimited dependence upon the influence of the heavens: for it is God that gives increase to the labours of both. *A spirit of earnest prayer should be the living soul of all your conduct.* While your eye is fixed upon the children, your heart should be lifted up to God. You should sit down as between them and the fountain of life, and while opening by instruction a channel to their hearts, seek to draw the living stream by prayer from heaven. Your *closet* should be the constant scene of your anxiety for their welfare. In those seasons of hallowed seclusion when your soul makes her nearest and happiest approaches to the throne of divine grace, give her in charge *their* immortal interests. God loves the prayers of his people, and especially delights in the prayers of pious benevolence. Importune him therefore to bless your efforts. Confess to him that the work of conversion is all his own. Hang the interests of the school upon his arm, and lay them down in the light of his countenance.

Especially *on the morning of the Sabbath*, in the prospect of your exertions, make the welfare of the children the principal subject of your prayers, alongside your own growth in grace. Pray for grace to be found faithful, and to be made sufficient for these things. Entreat of God to rouse you from lukewarmness, and to enable you to feel your responsibility for the souls of others. *There* qualify yourself, if I may so speak, for your office. It is astonishing what an effect is produced on our own feelings by fervent prayer. It elevates in our minds, and endears to our heart, every object which it embraces. It is not the pleading of a hireling advocate, who, after his most eloquent appeals, receives his fee, and forgets his client; but the intercession of genuine charity, which warms towards its object by its own impassioned entreaties on its behalf. Prayer will cherish all the tenderest sensibilities of the heart, and keep down the growth and influence of our natural selfishness. Were you to come to the school every Sabbath morning, like Moses from the Mount, direct from the presence and the converse of God, bringing all the solemn tenderness with which you had supplicated for the children at the mercy-seat, what a character would be imparted to your deportment! The solemn air of eternity irradiated with the beams of heavenly glory would be visible upon your countenance; while the meekness of Jesus, and the mercy of his Gospel, breathed forth in all your language, would admonish the children that it was not a time for them to trifle when their teacher had come to them with a "message from God."

Those who are most prayerful will be most successful, provided they possess other qualifications in an equal degree. On the other hand, it is a matter of little surprise that no success, in the way of spiritual benefit, attends the efforts of those by whom this duty is neglected. They labour, as might be expected, in a field on which the dew of heaven seldom distils, and which brings forth little other than thorns and briars. Whenever we shall be favoured to perceive a spirit of prayer resting upon the great mass of our teachers, and inspiring all their exertions, we shall not wait long before we hear of a degree of success among the children which will delight and astonish us; for it is said of Jehovah, that "He heareth prayer."

– 4 –

The Duties of Teachers to Each Other

IN every case of combined exertion, there devolve upon the co-workers, mutual obligations, on the due discharge of which the success of their efforts materially depends. This is obviously true as to the case in hand. Besides what is due to the children from the teachers, there is much to be observed by the teachers towards each other.

1. They should cultivate *a spirit of reciprocal affection*.

In addition to the ordinary reasons for brotherly love which exist in every case, your circumstances supply another of considerable weight. Unity of exertion certainly calls for unity of affection; for the former without the latter can exist but in a very feeble degree, and be crowned only with very partial success. Love should be the superintendent of every school. Affectionately devoted to the object of the institution, you should love everyone who contributes in the least measure to its success. Worldly and even wicked associations lead to strong affection between the united parties; the soldier contracts a strong affection for his comrade who fights by his side; the servant who is faithfully devoted to his master's interest feels a regard for his fellow-servant in whom he discovers the same fidelity; the traveller forms a growing friendship for the person, though accidentally met with on the road, with whom he shares the toils and dangers of the way; even a gang of robbers feel sometimes a sort of affection for each other. Certainly then a co-operation so benevolent in its objects as that in which you are engaged, and so holy in its acknowledged bond of union, ought to produce a high degree of Christian love. Labouring side by side in the cause of immortal souls, that cause in which the Saviour spent his life, and shed his blood; that cause which from beginning to end is emphatically the cause of love, you should cultivate towards each other no common measure of hallowed friendship. It is not enough that you avoid a state of open enmity; it is not enough that you maintain complaisant indifference, or cold and civil distance; this is very far below that cordial and glowing affection which should be cherished among the fellow-workers in such a cause. This should be the prompt and generous language of one heart to another, "I love you, for your love to these children, and the interests of piety." The teachers of every school should form a holy family, a devoted fraternity associated by the bond of affection for the purpose of benevolence, within whose sacred and peaceful circle, envy, jealousy, and strife should never be allowed a place; but which should incessantly exhibit the "good and pleasant sight of brethren dwelling together in unity."

2. There should be *cordial and general co-operation in everything which concerns the institution.*

The prosperity of *the school at large* is that which every individual teacher should keep in view, and which he should seek by the improvement of his own class. It is of vast importance that you should steadily and continually remember that, although you have separate and individual duties, yet you have no private and separate *interests.* The school forms a little community, of which you are a member, and to violate its integrity by setting up the interests of distinct parties, is treason. *You must all act together.* The worst of evils have arisen from the teachers being divided into little knots. These are frequently, perhaps generally, produced by the operation of private friendship. For example, there are two or three of the number who, from congeniality of mind or long intimacy, are on habits of the most friendly intercourse. Forgetting the consequences which are likely to result, they take no pains to conceal or suspend their intercourse during the time they are at the school; they are often seen talking to each other, and exchanging the warmest expressions of endeared friendship, while the rest are passed by with cold civilities or indifference. All this while a spirit of division is imperceptibly generated. Others, perceiving that they are not to be admitted to the select circle, form parties of their own. During the usual and uninterrupted routine of ordinary business, no effect peculiarly injurious perhaps arises; but the very first time that an offence occurs, or a diversity of opinion takes place, the mischief, which has been secretly collecting, explodes. Factions are formed according to the parties which had previously existed; opposition grows strong; the work of division and alienation goes forward; the seeds of lasting discord are sown, and the school receives an injury, from which it is long in recovering.

Take care, therefore, of forming the teachers into parties. Private friendships are not forbidden to you; but the school is not the place to display them. Even should you walk in company to the scene of your labours, remember to separate as friends the moment you touch the threshold of the school-room; and, suspending for a season all visible partialities, mingle with the whole body, and, feeling the pressure of a general bond, act upon the principle that you are *all one*.

Especially take care of systematically thinking and acting with a party. Endeavour in all cases of diversity of opinion to act independently and conscientiously. Be very watchful that your affections do not impose upon your judgement, and that your private attachments do not influence your public conduct: for if it be seen that in your official duties you act independently of personal regard, your friendships, however well known, will make no party, and do no harm.

3. *Never make the real or supposed faults of one teacher the matter of conversation with others.*

This rule equally extends to official delinquencies and personal offences. There is a most powerful propensity in human nature to what has been denominated with considerable propriety *backbiting;* or making the faults of an absent person the subject of conversation. This is a vice so mean, so mischievous, so cowardly; so characteristic of littleness as well as of malignity; that every holy man should hate it, and every wise man be ashamed of it. O what wisdom, what mercy, what love, is there in our Lord's directions! "If thy brother shall trespass against thee, go and tell him his fault between thee and him alone: if he shall hear thee, thou hast gained thy brother. But if he will not hear thee, then take with thee one or two more, that in the mouth of two or three witnesses every word may be established." (*Matthew 8:15, 16*). If this rule were universally obeyed, three quarters of the feuds and quarrels which destroy the peace, and desolate the temporal interests, of men would be cut off. "Tell him his fault between thee and him alone:" and of course this must mean tell *him first;* let not another know it until you have tried the effect of this private and personal representation. How often has the harmony of our schools been interrupted by a violation of this rule! A teacher's faults have been made the subject of free conversation, until the matter, swelled by falsehood and envenomed by malignity, has come to his ears in the most exasperating form. It is melancholy to reflect from what slight causes the most serious animosities have arisen, even among those who were professedly teaching a religion of forgiveness; and the grief is increased by considering what a small measure of forbearance would at one time have proved sufficient for preventing the whole series of the subsequent mischiefs. It is a difficult point to settle who is most to blame and most answerable for consequences; the person who first commits a fault, or he who by revenging or publishing it causes it to extend its baneful effects. If my neighbour be wanton or wicked enough to throw a kindled firebrand into my dwelling, and I, instead of immediately quenching it, throw it back into his premises, or cast it into the air for the wind to carry it whither it will, am I less answerable for the conflagration than he? So when you are offended by a brother teacher if, instead of going to him alone and endeavouring to come to an amicable adjustment of the affair, you throw back the firebrand in revenge, or cast it into the air by publicly talking of the matter, and a fiery contention ensues, you are perhaps the guiltier individual of the two.

Let me here enjoin upon all concerned in the active duties of a Sunday School, the diligent cultivation of that charity, or love, which the apostle has so exquisitely described in *1 Corinthians 13*: "Charity suffereth long," when injured, does not seek revenge; "charity is kind," is desirous of making everyone happy; "charity envieth not," feels no pain at the sight of another's excellences or possessions, nor dislikes him on that account; "vaunteth not itself," does not boast of what it has done or can do; "is not puffed up," has no proud conceit of its own attainments or achievements; "doth not behave unseemly," quietly discharges the duties of its own rank, station, age, or sex, without rudely stepping out of its own appropriate circle; "seeketh not her own," abhors selfishness; "is not easily provoked," is as backward to *take* offence, as it is to *revenge* it; "thinketh no evil," is willing to impute a good motive, until a bad one is proved; "rejoiceth not in iniquity, but rejoiceth in the truth," mourns the failings, and delights in the excellences, of her opponent; "beareth," or, as the word signifies, "covereth all things," covers with a mantle of love those faults which it is not necessary to disclose; "believeth all things," to the advantage of another; "hopeth all things," where there is scarcely evidence suffi-cient to induce belief; "endureth all things," is willing to make any sacrifice, and endure any privation, consistent with truth, in order to promote peace.

What schools we should have, under the control of such a spirit! What hinders us from cultivating this god-like, heavenly, and ever-lasting virtue, as the ruling temper of our hearts, and the all-pervad-ing spirit of the institution?

4. *Always address each other with kindness and respect.*

Avoid everything domineering, uncivil, and disrespectful, both in manner and in tone. It is greatly to be regretted, that suavity of speech and urbanity of manners appear to be regarded by some good people as almost heretical character traits. But I have yet to learn in what page of revelation courtesy is proscribed. Gold is not the less weighty for being burnished, nor the diamond less valuable for being polished; no, nor is real religion the less pure for being decorated with the ornament of real courtesy. The holiness of a saint receives no contamination or alloy from the manners of a gentleman.

I am not advocating the stiff cold etiquette of a heartless and cringing politeness, but that affectionate and respectful attention to each other's feelings which is made up of benevolence and good manners. "Let the law of kindness be in your lips, and your speech be always with grace;" remembering you are not many masters, but brethren.

It is of considerable importance that, as the children are required to respect their instructors, they should be invariably taught to do this by the example of the teachers mutually respecting each other. And as it is one object of Sunday School instruction, though not the ultimate one, to check what is rude, and polish what is rough, in the manners of the children, it is of no small consequence that, in the conduct of their teachers, they should constantly have before their eyes models of kindness and respect.

5. *Never interfere with the duties of each other.*

An officious meddling disposition is sure to do mischief and incur contempt. Your respective duties are sufficiently distinct to be clearly ascertained, and to render any encroachment inexcusable on the ground of ignorance. Upon observing any irregularity or neglect in the class of another, instead of attempting to rectify it yourself, mention it kindly to the teacher to whom the class belongs; especially remembering that the hint be given as privately and as delicately as possible, as no one should be convicted or reproved before his own pupils.

6. Be very careful to *discharge the general duties of your office in a manner suitable to your age, sex, and condition in life.*

Older and younger teachers are under reciprocal obligations to each other. Those whose years and experience entitle them to considerable deference from their younger fellow-labourers, should be exceedingly anxious to employ their seniority to great advantage. Let them remember the influence of their example, and not merely abstain from everything which it would be injurious for others to imitate, but abound in every virtue which may be copied with advantage. Unusual seriousness and zeal should characterise all their deportment. Connected with this should be *a friendly disposition to associate with their younger brethren.* There should be no distant, reserved, and repulsive behaviour, but a willingness to instruct, encourage, and guide them, without even a hint of a wish to dictate and govern. How eminently serviceable might such people render themselves by repressing intemperate zeal, by giving to youthful ardour a right direction, and smoothing the ruggedness with which the first stage in the career of usefulness is sometimes marked! Instead therefore of viewing the junior teachers as too young to be their associates, and leaving them to companions as inexperienced as themselves, let the senior labourers in this good cause consider them as objects commended to their especial protection; to be, under their fostering care, trained up to excellence in the duties of their office.

On the other hand, let the *younger teachers* be thoroughly aware of the duties of *their* age. Let them seek the company of their seniors; treat them with respect, solicit their advice, and hearken to their opinions with deference. Where youth is modestly inquisitive and age unostentatiously communicative, much benefit must result from their being brought into association. Young people, however, are exceedingly apt to be forward, flippant, positive, and self-confident. Nothing can be more offensive than to see a person, young in years, and still younger in experience, forgetful of the deference due to those who are wiser and older than himself, urging his own plans and views with a pertinacity scarcely tolerable in grey hairs, and in opposition to the ripe wisdom of his seniors, contending for their adoption as confidently as if he had received them by revelation from heaven. Modesty is a disposition so necessary in the character of youth that no talents can be a substitute for it, nor can any attainments, however splendid, be admitted as an excuse for the lack of it. Let those who have but recently entered upon their office always listen with great humility to those who have been employed in it for years, and eagerly avail themselves of the testimony of their experience. The worst of evils have arisen from that haughty temper which forgets that among equals in rank some are far better qualified than others, and that deference to them is no degradation.

Between the teachers of *opposite sexes* there are duties to be discharged which involve their own respectability, and the character of the institution. Some people, who understand no logic but that of the pocket, and who find it more cheap to find out the faults of an institution, than the means of its support, have sometimes made this objection against the plan of gratuitous teaching in our Sunday Schools, "that it gives occasion for too frequent meetings of young people, and often leads to hasty and injudicious connections in life." Leaving this insubstantial objection to pass like a shadow over a rock, I certainly see the necessity and importance of the most punctilious regard to all the rules of modesty and reserve, between male and female teachers. A school-room is not the place, nor is the Sabbath the time, for gossip between young men and women. Nothing can be more improper than to see young men intruding into an area set aside for the instruction of girls, and there nodding, laughing, or talking to a female acquaintance. Before an assembly of poor children, one of whose greatest dangers arises from a want of proper and delicate reserve between the sexes, and who are ready to copy with enthusiasm any want of decorum in their teachers, the very smallest deviation from the strict rules of propriety is a crime, not only against their manners, but against their morals. Under such circumstances, the most scrupulous circumspection is indispensably requisite.

And here, perhaps, it may be neither unseasonable nor unnecessary to caution young people against being led into ill-advised connections by the intercourse they necessarily must have with each other, after every rule of decorum has been observed. There exists no reason why a connection commenced at a Sunday School should necessarily be a bad one; nor, on the other hand, why it should necessarily be a good one. People may be very excellent teachers, and yet be very ill-adapted for husbands or wives. The qualifications required for these respective relationships are, in some respects, so essentially different, that there is no arguing from the one to the other.

Sometimes we shall find in the same school people of very *different standing in life;* and such a disparity, without an attention to the duties which it entails, is likely to be attended with some degree of discord. The richer and better-educated members of the little community should be careful to exclude from their conduct everything like the pride of station, and at the same time to avoid that insulting condescension, which makes its object feel at what a distance it is considered. It is a subtle and delicate point to distinguish between affability and familiarity; and to act with those who are below us in life, as fellow-labourers in the school, without making them our companions out of it.

Those whom Providence has destined to fill the *humbler stations of society*, and who are engaged in the work of tuition with others of more elevated circumstances, will also do well to guard against an obtrusive and forward disposition; without being servile, they should always be respectful. All they ought to expect from their superiors is, a kind co-operation in the duties of the school, without the familiarity of friends and companions in general.

7. *Prayer* is a duty which the teachers of a Sunday School mutually owe to each other.

If we are commanded to make supplications for all men, even for those with whom we have no other connection than such as is established by the common bond of humanity, surely those with whom we are united in the communion of Christian benevolence ought not to be excluded from our petitions. Mutual prayer, as I have already considered in the case of the children, would be productive of mutual endearment in proportion to its fervour. If on a Sabbath morning you devoted a portion of the time spent in the closet to entreat the blessing of God upon the persons and labours of your fellow-teachers, how sweetly would such an engagement prepare you to mingle with them in the duties of the day! Softened to benevolence by the exercises of piety, and with the fire of love still burning which prayer had kindled in your heart, with what a holy temper would you hasten to the scene of your exertions, and with what a glowing affection look round upon the objects of your fervent supplications! What an influence might it be expected such a system of mutual prayer, – sincerely, importunately and perseveringly presented, – would draw down from heaven upon the institution at large! Showers of blessings would come down in their season, in which both children and teachers would reciprocally rejoice. God hears and answers prayer; and of all the prayers which enter heaven, and rise before the throne, we can readily conceive that none more speedily catch His ear and move His hand than those which one Christian pours forth over the religious zeal of another; since such prayers are like the aromatic incense which ascended in a cloud before the mercy-seat, made up of many precious ingredients all of divine appointment.

-5-

The Temptations of Sunday School Teachers

A S this life is a state of probation, it may be reasonably expected that every situation will have its trials. Temptations vary with our circumstances; but there is no scene from which they are entirely excluded. The heavenly and the earthly paradise alternately witnessed their attack, their victory, and their havoc. Angelic as well as human perfection yielded to their shock, and left a warning to every subsequent age, "not to be high-minded, but to fear." In a world which God for a while has permitted to sink under the dominion of the prince of the power of the air, it is not to be wondered at that there is no situation in the church, however obscure and solitary, or however elevated, from which all temptation can be effectually shut out. The fact is, that, as our chief danger arises from our own evil heart, until we can be separated from our guilty selves, we shall look in vain for a spot sheltered from the attack of our spiritual enemies. Well did our merciful Redeemer know our weakness and our dangers, when He put into our lips that appropriate petition, "Lead us not into temptation."

What duty is more frequently enjoined in the New Testament than *watchfulness?* And what is more necessary? How incumbent this is on those who are engaged in the active duties of a Sunday School will be very apparent by even a partial summary of *their* temptations.

1. *They are in great danger of receiving injury to their own personal religion.*

The Sabbath, if the expression should not be thought too low, is the market-day of the soul, when she lays in the provisions which are to refresh her, and the materials which are to employ her, during the following week: if this day be misimproved, six days suffer for the neglect of one. It is very true that real godliness will not confine itself to peculiar times and places; but still there are both peculiar times and places which are eminently adapted to promote its life and power. The Sabbath and the sanctuary sustain the highest rank among the instituted means of religious benefit. It is *then* that the Christian, engaged in warfare with this world, like a ship in action with an enemy, lies by for a season to repair the damages he has received, and prepares again for action, by renewing the faith which gives him the victory. It is then that piety, wearied and weakened by the toils of her journey, sits down to rest beneath the shadow of Christ's ordinances, and, refreshing herself at the river of life which flows at her feet, rises with renovated strength to pursue her course to the city of habitation. Hence all those who are concerned for the prosperity of their spiritual interests, and are wise in the selection of means to promote them, set a high value upon the Sabbath as the chief auxiliary of true religion.

Now, without great care, a Sunday School teacher is in imminent danger of losing much of the benefit of the Christian Sabbath. As your attendance is required pretty early at the school, you are often exposed to the temptation of neglecting secret prayer on the Sunday morning. Without a most resolute and self-denying habit of early rising, you will be very frequently hurried away to the school before you have had time, except in a very hasty manner, to supplicate a blessing from God upon the services of the day. A Sabbath commenced without prayer is likely to be spent without pleasure, and closed without profit. It is in the closet that the soul is prepared for the blessings of the sanctuary; it is there the understanding is cleared for instruction, and the heart softened for impression; it is there that God excites the spiritual hunger and thirst which he afterwards intends to satisfy with the provisions of his holy temple. Everyone who wishes to find the Sabbath a delight, should introduce it by a season of earnest and secret prayer, which you, without most determined habits of early rising, are likely, in consequence of your engagements, to neglect.

Without great vigilance you are in danger of *losing the spirituality of the Sabbath altogether, and making it rather a day of business than of devotion.* In many large schools much of the Lancasterian system of education is introduced into the method of instruction, which certainly facilitates the communication of knowledge; but at the same time it must be confessed that, from its nature, it has a tendency, unless there be pre-eminent care on the part of the teacher, to increase the secularising influence of the whole business of instruction. The audible repetition of orders, the movement of the classes, the exhibition of signals, and indeed the whole mechanism of the plan has a great tendency to destroy that tranquillity and spirituality of mind which are essential to the exercises of devotion. In addition to this, the little vexations and irritations which the conduct of the scholars so frequently produce, are very apt to disturb and discompose the most amiable temper, and thus disqualify the soul for the enjoyment of religion, which requires the most serene and unruffled atmosphere. The body, too, often grows weary, and the animal spirits flag; under such circumstances you sometimes enter upon the means of grace but ill-prepared to benefit by them.

The service passes on, while alas neither the solemnity of prayer, nor the animating notes of holy praise, neither the fervour of the preacher, nor the seriousness of the surrounding congregation, seems to interest or impress you; and then, mourning the coldness and barrenness of your heart, you retire to mark upon the gloomy chronicle of misimprovement another Sabbath lost. Many a teacher will subscribe to the truth of this representation by a deep and heavy sigh; and many a tongue be ready to exclaim, "My wasting piety yields sad proof that, without watchfulness, genuine godliness may receive lamentable injury even in a Sunday School. But tell me how I may guard against the danger: its existence I know without being told."

Begin the day with earnest prayer that you may carry a devotional spirit to your labours. Seriously remember your danger, and diligently watch against it. Keep in view the ultimate object of your exertions, and elevate your views from the mere communication of knowledge to the salvation of immortal souls; as long as you can fix your mind on the spiritual interests of the children, and labour affectionately for them, you guard against the secularising influence of the ordinary school business, and are cherishing a spirit in every way friendly to your own piety. Make it the subject of earnest supplication that God would preserve you from the danger to which you are exposed. Endeavour to acquire settled habits of stillness and order, that all unnecessary bustle may be avoided, and everything conducted with calmness and serenity. Employ in devotional retirement the time you have to spare during the intervals of public worship. By these means assiduously applied the spirit of true piety may be preserved; and personal religion remain uninjured amidst the routine of Sunday School instruction.

There is another source from which some degree of danger may be expected, and that is *a habit of speaking on religious subjects with too much indifference and levity*. This applies to everyone who is called to teach religion officially. The solemn topics of heavenly truth can never be treated lightly with impunity. A mind accustomed to dwell upon them in a mere official and unfeeling manner, must gradually lose its susceptibility to their living influence; and become hardened against their power to sanctify and comfort. That which at one time we treat as the ordinary routine of business, it will be difficult at another to enjoy as the element of devotion. Let us then take care never to handle the truths of revelation with a light and careless temper; for by such means they are likely to become "the savour of death unto death." "The solemn awe, which warns us how we touch a holy thing," should ever permeate our minds while our tongues are engaged upon the affairs of eternity. Never forget that everlasting interests hang upon the truths which you teach to the children, and that their manner of learning them will, in a considerable measure, be in imitation of your manner of teaching them.

There is the greater need of watching against the danger to which your office as a teacher exposes your own personal piety; as of all causes of spiritual declension, this is the most likely to be excused by a deceived conscience. Is the following mode of reasoning new to you? "It is true I have not been of late so attentive to personal religion as I formerly was, and it must be confessed that divine truths affect me less powerfully than they once did: but as the neglect was produced by an attention to the interests of others, it is quite pardonable; for if I have not kept my own vineyard, I have kept the vineyard of others; and therefore I consider that my falling off a little should be considered rather in the light of a sacrifice, than a sin." It becomes us to recollect that our first care is with our own soul; and that, as no duties can be incompatible with each other, nothing is required of us that *necessarily* interferes with personal religion. Nothing can possibly be a substitute for this; nothing excuse the decline of it. Neither the most diffusive benevolence, nor the most ardent zeal, will be admitted by God as an apology for sinking into the crime of lukewarmness. There is however no *necessary* connection between a decay of piety and the duties of a Sunday School: the danger arises only in cases in which there is a lack of caution. Properly conducted, your employment would be found rather an auxiliary, than a foe, to the greatest spirituality of mind.

2. Another temptation to which Sunday School teachers are exposed, is *a spirit of pride*.

To be a teacher of others; to be invested with authority; to be regarded as an oracle; to be listened to with deference; to say to one, "Come," and he cometh, to another, "Go," and he goeth, even among children, is a situation which has its temptations, and which some weak minds have found quite too powerful for their *humility*. You mistake, if you suppose the distinction and elevation of *your* office are too inconsiderable to induce pride. Pride is a vice that does not dwell exclusively in kings' houses, wear only soft raiment, and feed sumptuously every day upon lofty titles, fame, or affluence; generated in the depravity of our nature, it accommodates itself to our circumstances, and adapts itself to our notions; it is found as often in the cottage as in the mansion; and where it has never tasted the rich fare of loftier elevations, feeds with avidity upon the lowest distinctions which raise one man above another. Consciousness of superiority, whatever be the object of comparison, is the element of this most hateful disposition; and this may be supplied even from the office of a Sunday School teacher. The danger is greatly increased where the talents of a young person have procured for him a prominent station, and assigned to him the discharge of extraordinary duties.

It would indeed be an unhappy abuse of the system, if it should be perverted into a means of destroying that modest and retiring disposition which is the most becoming ornament of the young, and rendering them bold, forward, and conceited. And it requires no penetration to discern that some danger of this must ever attend a season of extraordinary activity like that in which we live. The mode of doing good in the present age, with all its incalculable advantages to the interests of mankind, needs the greatest watchfulness, both on the part of principal agents and subordinate instruments, lest it generate the disposition against which this admonition is directed. Vast multitudes are now brought from silence and obscurity to enjoy a share of that distinguished honour which the cause of Christ imparts to the meanest of its advocates. Let them therefore be watchful over their own spirits; for the loss of humility from the Christian character leaves a deficiency not to be supplied by the most splendid talents or the most active zeal; and it would be an evil which our congregations would have cause to deplore with tears of blood, if their junior members should ever by any cause be inflated with the spirit of pride.

3. Nearly allied to this is the danger of acquiring *a dogmatical, authoritative, and overbearing manner*.

The last particular referred to *disposition*, this relates to *demeanour* only; and through the force of habit a person may fail in the latter without being considerably infected by the former. Accustomed to speak with authority to the children, and to expect prompt obedience to your commands, you are in danger, without great watchfulness, of carrying the tone and air of office into your general deportment. A habit of this kind may be formed by imperceptible degrees, and displayed without consciousness, and if contracted it will not be broken without difficulty. Wherever it exists, it never fails to create disgust, but is never so disgusting as in young people.

– 6 –

The Discouragements
of Sunday School Teachers

EVERY cause which is worth supporting will have to encounter difficulties; and they are generally proportionate to the value of the object to be accomplished. The career of benevolence is not a path of flowers, leading down a gentle declivity, where the philanthropist treads softly and swiftly without a difficulty to check his progress, or a discouragement to chill his ardour. Mercy has far more to obstruct her course than even justice, since the latter is attended by the strong arm of power, to resent injuries offered to her dignity, and remove obstacles opposing her progress: whereas mercy, accompanied only by that wisdom which is peaceable, must attempt to do by gentleness what she cannot effect by force; must toil through difficulties which she cannot remove; under the most aggravated injuries, must console herself with the thought that she did not deserve them; amidst present discouragement, must cheer herself with the hope of future success; and after waiting long and patiently for the fruit of her labours, will sometimes find her only reward in the purity of her intentions and the consciousness of having done all she could.

The faithful teacher will meet with many discouragements, which I will now describe, and endeavour to prevent.

1. Your discouragement will arise frequently from *defects in the children's minds*.

Instead of finding them quick in their conceptions, and steady in their application, you will often find them volatile in their habits, and *slow of apprehension*. After toiling several weeks in teaching them the alphabet, you will in some cases have the mortification to find that little progress has been made, and months elapse before much visible improvement takes place. In looking round upon your class, you will sometimes exclaim with a sigh of despondency, "So long have I been labouring to instruct that boy, and yet to the present hour he can scarcely add syllable to syllable. It is like ploughing upon a rock, and sowing on sand. I feel almost inclined to abandon the work altogether." Never yield to such feelings. Innumerable instances have occurred, in which the dullest children in the school have ultimately become the teacher's richest reward. Plants of great excellence are often of slow growth, and repay with ample interest the gardener's heavy toil and delayed expectations. And even should no such result crown your efforts, still bear with their dullness, recollecting that this very circumstance renders them more in need of your benevolent regard.

Their *ingratitude* is oftentimes exceedingly discouraging. Aware of the costly sacrifices you make, and the incessant labour you endure, for their benefit, you expect in them a just sense of their advantages, and a grateful acknowledgment of their obligations. Instead of this, you often see them utterly destitute of both; trifling over their privileges as if they were worth nothing to them, and as thankless towards you as if it cost you nothing to impart them. Perceiving that your kindness is wasted upon objects which it fails to impress, you feel sometimes disposed to withdraw exertions so little valued and improved. But consider, this very state of the children's minds, instead of inducing you to relax your exertions, should stimulate you to greater activity, since it is a part of that depravity of heart and deformity of character for the removal of which they are entrusted to your care. To abandon them on this account would be like a physician giving up his patient because he is diseased. The more ignorant and ungrateful you find them, the more should you labour for their improvement, since those vices, if not reformed in childhood, are likely to attain a dreadful maturity in future life.

The small degree of their improvement operates very unfavourably upon the minds of their instructors. Who has not sometimes experienced a chilling depression when he has looked round upon the school, and compared the actual state of the children with the advantages they have enjoyed? How common are such reflections as these: "Alas! how few of these children appear at present to be the better, as to any moral improvement, for the instructions they have received! How few have received any serious impressions, or imbibed any religious principles! How many appear as depraved as when they entered the school, and are leaving it without a single proof on which a teacher can rest his hope that they are really the better for his instructions! And even of those who at one time seemed to promise well, how few are there whose budding excellences have escaped the corrupting influence of bad example! Disappointed so often, we are afraid to indulge another expectation. Where are the boasted advantages of Sunday School instruction? Where the general improvement of mind, of manners, and of heart, for which we have been waiting? The present generation of the poor seems to be growing up as vicious and immoral as any that are past. We have almost laboured in vain, and spent our strength for nought. It amounts well-nigh to a question with us, whether we may not relinquish our efforts without any serious injury to the interests of morality or religion."

This is the dark side of the picture: but it has a bright one, which should check these discouraging fears, and resist the paralysing influence they are calculated to cherish. That in a great majority of cases no present visible effect of a religious kind is produced, I admit; but equally obvious it is that in not a few instances the following happy result has been witnessed. If you could look at the aggregate of success which has already followed similar exertions, you would behold a scene which would fix your attention in silent wonder, or raise your heart to transports of delight. It is a fact which abundant evidence confirms that multitudes of children have already been converted to God, blessed for both worlds, and made happy for eternity, by means of Sunday School instruction. At the very moment when you are giving vent to the sighs of disappointment, and yielding to the influence of despondency, a thousand harps are struck in heaven by a band of glorified spirits who received their first devout impressions in a Sunday School. Could you listen to their harmony, and gaze upon their beauty: could you witness the seraphic glow which is diffused over their frames, and hear the rapturous praises which they pour forth to Him that sits upon the throne, as often as they repeat the honoured name of their beloved teacher; before such a scene discouragement would instantly vanish, and animating hope would fill its place. When you feel despondency creeping through your soul, send your imagination for one of those heavenly harpers, and let her charm away the gloomy thoughts of your troubled breast by the song of her conversion.

On the way to heaven, as well as *within its gates*, are a goodly company, redeemed from their vain conversation within the limits of a Sunday School. Scarcely a Christian church will be found in the kingdom which has had such an institution under its care, but records some members who by its means were converted from the error of their ways. The number of living witnesses, who from heartfelt experience can bear their testimony to the spiritual benefit of this system, would fill several of our largest places of public worship.

In addition to this, numberless instances of *external reformation* have occurred, and many who would otherwise have been running to excess or riot, have been trained to habits of morality, industry, and order.

In many cases, the seed of the kingdom begins to germinate long before your eye discerns the hidden process. A secret work is going on, which shall one day surprise and delight you. The first dawn of day commences amidst the thickest shades of night; the tide begins to turn long before it is observed by a person walking upon the shore; thus the initial stage of conversion is often hidden amidst the remains of unregeneracy from every eye but His who sees in secret. When you are most discouraged, there may be the least cause for it.

Even those unhappy youths whose conduct excludes all joy for the present, and almost all hope for the future, even they, at some distant time, may yield a rich harvest from the seed which is now, with respect to them, sown in tears. The instructions you communicate can never be totally forgotten. They give light and power to the conscience; keep the mind in a state of susceptibility to devout impression; and render the heart more fit to be acted upon by those incidents of a providential nature which are continually occurring to arrest the sinner in his career. In the gloomy season of distress, when reflection can be resisted no longer, then what they were taught in the school may be brought vividly to their remembrance. Then, when no preacher and no friend is near, conscience may recall the terrors of the law, and memory the glad tidings of the Gospel, until the poor trembling sinner, amidst the long-neglected stores that were deposited in her mind at the Sunday School, finds the means of her conviction, conversion, and consolation.

It may be also observed, that minds trained in the knowledge of the Gospel are far more likely than others to benefit by preaching. They have a clearer understanding of sermons. Besides, as it is through the mind that God converts the heart, they are in a fairer way to derive spiritual impressions than those who have lived in brutish ignorance. This is a species of advantage arising from Sunday School instruction not sufficiently thought of. The teacher is unquestionably a powerful auxiliary to the preacher, and the success of the latter in many cases must in justice be shared by the former. You may therefore check the despondency of your hearts by this consideration, that where no present visible effect is produced by your instructions, you may by a division of labour in the business of conversion be preparing for this great change being afterwards effected under the instrumentality of the minister.

Children in whose hearts devout impressions may have been produced are often removed from beneath your care before you have an opportunity to witness the fruit of your toil; but the eye of God is upon His own work, and He will one day make known to you all that He does by you.

As to the discouragement which arises from the general appearance of the lower orders of society, it should be recollected that a mighty change indeed must be wrought before it becomes visible in the aggregate; this ought not to be expected until the system has had another generation or two to work upon the mass of the poor with the weight of accumulated benefit. Thousands and thousands of instances of individual conversion and reformation may be effected, without at present altering the *visible* condition of the poor in general. Wickedness is noisy and obtrusive, and may be seen and heard in every place of concourse: piety is silent, modest, and retiring; not lifting up her voice in the street, nor praying at the corners of the streets. One murder makes more noise than a hundred conversions. To see the abounding of wickedness, the overflowing of ungodliness, we need not give ourselves the trouble of research; but to witness the good effects of Sunday Schools, we must follow the subjects of them to the closet of devotion, and to the retired scenes of domestic life and social order, where, like the violet, they are to be traced rather by their fragrance than their colours, and are valued in private more than they are known in public.

2. A second source of discouragement is often found in *the conduct of the children's parents.*

It is extremely disheartening to meet with so little co-operation as is generally afforded by them: this, however, should produce double exertions on your part, by convincing you that the children are cast entirely on your mercy for religious and moral improvement.

The same *ignorance* and *ingratitude* as are displayed by the children, are also in many cases manifested by their parents. It is not uncommon to meet with people so unthinking and thankless as to talk of conferring obligations upon us by sending their children to our schools. Such monstrous ingratitude is exceedingly trying to benevolence, and sometimes nearly extinguishes it. Let not the children however suffer for the sins of their parents. Continue to cherish their interests, and promote their welfare, notwithstanding every discouragement. Remember, you profess that your efforts are perfectly gratuitous; and therefore, to be consistent, you should make them dependent upon no wages, not even the effusions of a grateful heart. Do good for its own sake, and let your reward arise from the consciousness of doing it. "A good man shall be satisfied from himself." Imitate the conduct of your adorable Redeemer, who ever went about doing good, amidst ignorance and ingratitude, sufficient, one should have thought, to make infinite mercy itself weary in well-doing.

3. Sometimes you are cast down by *the unconcern which is manifested by the senior and more respectable members of the church.*

It can never be sufficiently deplored that so large a fund of knowledge, wisdom, and experience as is to be found in the senior branches of many of our congregations should be entirely withheld from benefitting the children; and the regret is considerably increased by observing the total indifference with which such people frequently regard the whole concerns of the school. This arises from a mistaken idea that these things belong exclusively to the young. Is there anything, I would ask, in this business, which would render it a disgrace for the most affluent, aged, or pious members of our churches to display a solicitude in its prosperity? Did the Saviour of the world interest Himself in the care of young children, and can *any one* of His followers think such a concern beneath him? I am not now asking the aged to sit down upon the bench of the young, or to sustain the toils of labour amidst the infirmities of age. I am not urging the father to neglect the souls of his own offspring in order to instruct the children of the stranger. All I ask, all I wish, is, that they would discover a lively and constant concern for the welfare of the school, and give it as much of their time and attention as their strength will allow, and prior claims admit. The hoary crown of righteous old age occasionally seen within the precincts of the school sheds a lustre upon the institution, and encourages the ardour of youthful breasts. The children are awed, the teachers are animated by the occasional assistance of men whose standing in the church and ripened piety command respect. Where however this is unhappily denied, and the young are left without the counsel and smiles of their seniors, instead of yielding to discouragement, endeavour by your own renewed exertions to remedy the evil and supply the defect. The less others care for the children, the more anxiety to be diligent should operate in your heart.

4. The mind of a teacher is very often discouraged by *the want of efficient co-operation in his fellow-labourers.*

Perhaps you are lamenting that your co-workers are either too few in number, or lamentably defective in suitable qualifications. Plans of usefulness which you know are adapted to promote the great end, are opposed or counteracted by the ignorance and stubbornness of your fellow-teachers. You are left almost to struggle alone, you cannot do the things you would. Thwarted and impeded, you are often ready to quit the field where your operations are cramped, and your usefulness diminished. This circumstance, instead of being a reason for your resignation, should operate as a very powerful inducement for your continuance. The fewer there are to carry on the school, or the more slender their qualifications, the more criminal would it be in you to retire. This would be to forsake the cause in its emergency, and take your place amongst those who are its friends only in its prosperity. Nothing can be more noble than to see a man struggling the more for a benevolent object the more he is opposed by some and neglected by others; this is the glory and triumph of great minds, heroism in the cause of mercy. Perseverance may bring its reward by collecting round you, in process of time, a band of like-minded labourers, who will rejoice to put themselves under the direction of such a leader.

– 7 –

The Preservation of Zeal in Sunday School Teachers

IT is a fact which all experience proves, that the most important object, by being constantly in sight, loses much of its power to interest. Zeal is apt to languish when it is no longer excited by the stimulus of novelty; and the fervour of first love, without great care, will soon sink into dull formality. It is not to be wondered at, if among the active supporters of a Sunday School, the vice of luke-warmness should sometimes be found. Hence it is of importance to ascertain the best means for keeping up the spirit of the teacher's office. By this, I mean, *the prosecution of its duties with vigour, interest, and delight,* in opposition to that lifeless and indolent manner of dragging through them which is but too common with many.

1. *Keep in view the ultimate object of your labours.*

The more importance we attach to an object, the less we shall be exposed to the danger of ceasing to regard it with concern. Whatever is momentous must be interesting. Hence the necessity of keeping steadily and clearly before your mind the salvation of the soul as the ultimate end of all your efforts. What can have such a tendency to engage the feelings, and keep them engaged, as this? The mere endeavour to teach how to read, the effort at only intellectual improvement, cannot, in the very nature of things, have such power over the heart of the teacher, as the steady contemplation of the immortal soul; salvation is a noble prize, and eternity a wonderful excitement. If anything can keep up the spirit of the office, it is to bring the mind regularly under the influence of such inducements as these. When you feel your heart losing its ardour, and sinking into a lukewarm state, look afresh to the world of immortality, and behold in the crown of eternal life the object of your pursuit. If anything can keep alive your attention to the interests of the children, it will be the constant repetition of this sentiment, "I am seeking their everlasting salvation."

2. *Well-conducted Sunday School Unions* have a powerful tendency to promote the spirit of your office.

The occasional meeting of fellow-labourers from different schools, together with the interesting communications and mutual exhortations which are then delivered, have a very enlivening effect. The very sight of so large a body of fellow-teachers, engaged in the same cause, has an exhilarating tendency, especially when one and another details the result of successful exertions. Not only do neighbouring flames brighten each other's blaze, but even dying embers are rekindled when brought into contact. So the communion which is established by these associations promotes, in a very powerful manner, the feeling essential to the character of a good teacher. A holy emulation is also excited, which, so long as it does not degenerate into envy, leads on to the happiest effects. The annual meetings, which are necessarily connected with the Union, aid the general impression, and keep up the interest in an eminent degree. It has been universally admitted by those who have tried the plan that it is full of advantages in respect of the particular object which I am now considering. The teachers who are connected with the best regulated Unions can testify, from ample experience, to their adaptation to keep up the spirit of the office.

I must, however, repeat what I have already stated in the Introduction, that, without great watchfulness, the effects of Unions will upon experience be found to be of a mixed character. They have in some instances tended to produce and cherish a spirit of confederation and faction among the teachers, who, regarding themselves as a separate and independent body, have disturbed the churches to which they belonged by the consequence they assumed, and the authority they claimed. The array of numbers as presented at the meetings of these associations, and especially the intercourse to which this sometimes leads with people of turbulent dispositions, are likely to give a consciousness of strength and importance to those who, on a less wide and conspicuous field of action, would have retained all their original humility and modesty.

3. *Occasional meetings among the teachers of the same school for conversation and prayer* in immediate reference to their joint labours, are exceedingly beneficial.

At these meetings everything should be communicated which individual experience in instruction has proved to be at all calculated for general encouragement. Each one should feel himself under obligation to render such friendly interactions as interesting as he can, by making known everything of an instructive or stimulating nature connected with Sunday Schools, which he had seen, heard, or read; but especial care must be taken that nothing be done for the sake of vainglory or pride, for to have such meetings converted into occasions for display would effectually counteract their beneficial influence.

4. *Ministerial assistance in the way of exhortation, inspection, and advice*, would powerfully contribute to keep up the true spirit of the office. [1]

---

1. It is a matter of great surprise and equal regret, that many ministers appear to take little or no interest in the concerns of the Sunday Schools supported by their congregations. They are scarcely ever to be seen among the children, or affording their presence and instruction at the meetings of the teachers. The annual sermon which they preach for the benefit of the institution seems to be regarded by them as a legal discharge from all further obligation to take any interest in it; and it is neglected and forgotten until they sit down to compose their sermon for the next anniversary. To what can such an omission be attributed? They can scarcely imagine that a school containing two, three, or four hundred immortal souls, is an object below their notice, or beyond their duty; nor will they shelter themselves under the excuse that when they undertook the charge of the congregation, they did not stipulate to concern themselves about the school. Does it comport with that zeal and piety by which they profess to be moved, to hear of so many immortal

Engage your respective ministers to meet you occasionally in your social interviews, that, by the breath of animated exhortation, they may fan the expiring spark, and feed the holy fire. Accustomed to public admonition, they know how to touch the springs of action, and to awaken the dormant energies of the human mind. It is no pride in me to say, that if a minister's heart be engaged in the work, and he be respected by his people, he has it in his power to awaken an interest in the minds of the teachers which scarcely anything else can supply. Use every means therefore to engage his zealous concern in the welfare of the institution.

5. *A constant perusal of publications that relate to Sunday School instruction*, especially the details of successful exertion, would be exceedingly useful.

Any particular taste is vigorously stimulated by the perusal of books that focus on its appropriate subject. Be ever watchful therefore to meet with new information and facts illustrative of the advantages of the work in which you are engaged. You rise from reading an encouraging anecdote with fresh eagerness. You see what others do, and how they do it: and while you are directed you are also excited. I recommend, with peculiar earnestness, the *Teacher's Magazine*, already alluded to in the Introduction, as eminently adapted to preserve in your breast the true spirit of your office.

souls, most of them grossly ignorant and wicked, assembling every week within the sphere of their labours, for religious instruction, and yet scarcely ever to inquire how they are going on? Do not ministers strangely neglect the means of increasing their own personal influence when they allow so important an institution to be in constant operation among their people, and yet have little or no share in directing its movements? Is it not teaching their congregations to act independently of their pastors, and to diminish the weight of their office, which is already in the estimation of many far too light? Do they consult the interests of the church by neglecting those of the Sunday School? If a proper share of attention were given to those poor youths, in all probability its happy result would often prove a balm to heal the wounds occasioned by a want of ministerial success. Here they would find materials to build up their dilapidated churches, and strengthen the walls of Zion, long mouldering beneath the desolating ravages of death. It is true, in many cases the pastor's hands are already nearly full of cares, and his arms weighed down with the interests dependent upon them; but the duty I enjoin would add little to the number or the weight of his engagements, while it would add much to his influence, his usefulness, and his comfort.

6. *An imitation of the best examples* will promote the same end.

In every school we shall find some whose superior qualifications and zeal entitle them to be considered as models. Instead of observing them with envy, mark them with admiration, cultivate their acquaintance, and endeavour by the glowing ardour of *their* spirit, to rekindle the fervour of your own.

7. Occasionally *devoting a portion of time to examine the state of your mind in reference to your duties* would be a means of improvement.

The true spirit of religion is very powerfully assisted by extraordinary seasons of devotion. The attention is more arrested and fixed by what is unusual than by what occurs in the ordinary routine of customary engagements. Half an hour occasionally devoted to a serious examination of the state of your heart in reference to the object you have embraced, when you can deliberately survey its magnitude, ascertain the manner in which it should be regarded, recollect the way in which it has been pursued by you, rouse your zeal from its slumber, and stimulate your heart to fresh activity, will be attended with the happiest effects.

It should be impressed upon all minds, that there is in the human spirit a lamentable propensity to lukewarmness, which can be effectually roused only by a violent and perpetual struggle with ourselves.

To all that I have enjoined should be added a constant supplication at the throne of divine grace, that God by His Holy Spirit, would keep alive in your hearts those feelings of holy benevolence and pious zeal, in which the spirit of the office essentially consists.

– 8 –
Motives to Diligence

IF in addition to what has been already advanced, anything be still wanting to stimulate your zeal, yield to the influence of the following motives.

1. *Dwell upon the value of Sunday Schools to all the present interests of society.*

As Britons and as Christians you must love the country that gave you birth; and that man is unworthy to tread the soil, or breathe the air, of Britain, who is unconscious of the blessings of this "bright speck upon the bosom of the ocean." Now, if we love our country, we must desire to see her great amidst the nations of the earth, safe amidst her greatness, and happy in her safety. And who needs to be informed that wisdom and knowledge must be the stability of her times? Her greatness, her safety, and her happiness, all rest upon the moral character of her population. Whatever elevates this, exalts the nation. Next to the labours of an evangelical ministry, no plan that ever was devised has a greater tendency to improve the religious state of society than the institution of Sunday Schools.

They lessen the crimes which disturb its peace. It is to be recollected that the instruction communicated by you is strictly *moral* and

religious. How far mere general knowledge, independently of revelation, would operate in improving the moral character of a people,
we can scarcely presume to determine, because the experiment has
never been tried; but that the communication of *religious* knowledge has a more beneficial tendency, it would be a waste of time and
ridiculous to attempt to prove. It may be useful, however, to remind
you here of those great national facts which are so often appealed to
in illustration of the good effects of religious education among the
poor. It is generally known and allowed that Scotland, and the lower
counties of it in particular, are distinguished from all other parts
of the British empire, by the attention which is bestowed on early
education, and the provision which is made for the wide and regular diffusion of its benefits. It is provided by law in Scotland, that
there shall be a school established, and a master appointed, in every
parish. Many additional schools are also founded by donations and
legacies: so that in the southern parts of that kingdom, it is very rare
to find a person who cannot both read and write; and it is deemed
scandalous not to be possessed of a Bible. Now, what are the effects
of this upon the national character and habits of the Scotch, and on
their morals and social order? It is principally owing to this, says
Mr Howard the philanthropist, that the numerous emigrants from
that country, dispersed over almost all Europe, appear with credit,
and advance themselves in their several stations. From the tables
of the same justly celebrated writer, it appears that in the whole of
Scotland, whose population, at the time of his calculations, was esti-
mated to amount to at least one million six hundred thousand souls,
only one hundred and thirty-four people were convicted of capital
crimes in a period of nineteen years; being, on the average, about
seven in each year. In a subsequent table we are informed, that in
the single circuit of Norfolk in England, including six counties, and
containing, it is supposed, not more than eight hundred thousand
people, being but half of the population of Scotland, no less than
four hundred and thirty-four criminals were condemned to death in
the space of twenty-three years; which is an annual average of nearly
nineteen capitally convicted; besides eight hundred and seventy-four
sentenced to transportation. There is thus a difference in favour of
Scotland, in this important point, in the ratio of seven to thirty-eight.

And it should be observed, that the education in Scotland to which this superiority may be attributed includes to a great extent training in morality and religion, although there is reason to fear that of late years some relaxation has taken place.

If we pass over to Ireland we shall find the darkest part of the empire with respect to religious education, the most fruitful of crimes and miseries. The wretched state of that unhappy country is in a considerable degree to be traced up to the prevalence of a religion which, with its characteristic cruelty, withholds the Bible from the poor.

Consider then what benefits you are conferring upon society by promoting the religious education of the poor. But besides preventing crimes recognised in law, you are the happy instruments of lessening the prevalence of that host of vices which, although amenable only to the bar of God, convulse society to its centre, and spread distraction and misery through all its walks. Profanity and falsehood, drunkenness and debauchery, excessive rage and ungoverned malignity, and all the dispositions that in the different social relations render man a fiend to man, it may be reasonably hoped, are considerably diminished by the influence of your benevolent exertions.

On the other hand *Sunday Schools multiply the virtues that establish the comfort of society*. All the particular duties that arise out of the reciprocal ties of society are taught, particularly the general principles of benevolence and submission, which like two mighty columns support the whole fabric of our social interests. Although the general aspect of society in its lower classes appears as yet unchanged, and the wintry face of its morality at present seems to defer to a distant period the harvest of your zeal, still let it be a stimulus to your exertions to be assured that you are pouring the principle of fertility through a thousand channels, and that already you see here and there a vernal flower lifting its head amidst barrenness and storms, the welcome harbinger of a happier season. Already innumerable masters bless your labours for faithful servants: wives pour out their gratitude for industrious and affectionate husbands; and children as, well clad, well fed, well taught, they gather round the knees of a kind and tender father, turn with the thankful smiles of their happiness to you, as their benefactors, who made their parents what they are. Society through all its ranks gratefully acknowledges the obligations conferred by your labours, and earnestly solicits their continuance. The King from his throne, and the Parliament in both houses, have paid the tribute of admiration to the utility of your exertions. You are admitted to be some of the best friends of the community, and the most efficient benefactors of the poor. Your efforts are directed to prevent crimes instead of punishing them, and to prevent misery instead of merely relieving it. Pursue your labours with increased diligence, since their tendency is to strengthen the foundations and adorn the fabric of society.

2. Dwell upon the incalculable worth of immortal souls.

So far as the children are individually concerned, I again remind you that their temporal interests are the *lowest* object of your pursuit. Your last and highest end is the salvation of the immortal soul. This is your aim, to be instrumental in converting the souls of the children from the error of their ways, and training them up in the fear of God, for glory everlasting. What an object! The immortal soul! the salvation of the human spirit! The soul was the last and noblest work of God in the formation of the world; the finish and ornament of this material fabric, on which the divine Architect bestowed his most mature deliberation, and expended his richest treasures. It stood amidst creation the beauteous image of its Creator. This was the object which first caught the envious eye of Satan upon his expulsion from heaven, and in the spoils of which his malice sought a fiend-like solace. The fall of the soul dragged the whole creation with it into the vortex of ruin. The salvation of the soul was selected by the great God in the councils of eternity to be the means of exhibiting to the universe the most glorious display of his own perfections, on which mercy, wisdom and power were to exhaust their united resources. The value of the soul was such that the Son of God could justify himself to all worlds, as not degrading his dignity, or disparaging his wisdom, when for its salvation he veiled his divinity in human flesh, was for a while made lower than the angels, tabernacled amidst the sorrows of mortality, and closed a life of humiliation and suffering upon the ignominious cross. On the redemption of the soul all the revelations of heaven, and all the dispensations of grace, all the labours of prophets, priests and apostles, were lavished. The conversion of a soul stirs the angels to action, and draws them with tender concern to minister to its safety. What then must be the value of the human soul? Now you see the justice of our Saviour's language: "What is a man profited if he gain the whole world, and lose his own soul? or what shall a man give in exchange for his soul?' Now you perceive this is no hyperbole; and that literally the globe, weighed against the value of one human spirit, is less than the small dust of the balance. Convert the sun into one blazing diamond, the moon into a pearl, and every star that decks the firmament into a gem, all bear no proportion to the value of the soul. Arithmetic, with all its powers, is here of no use; it cannot aid our conceptions. Think of the *immortality* of the soul, and this one property of its nature raises it above all calculation. It is in consequence of *this* that it has been said with justice, that the salvation of a soul secures a greater sum of happiness than the temporal deliverance of an empire for a thousand ages; for the latter will come to an end, but not the former. By the same argument, the loss of one soul is a greater catastrophe than the total sum of all the temporal misery endured upon the face of the globe from the period of the fall to the general conflagration. Say now, is not such an object worthy of all the means that are or can be employed for its attainment? Do you hesitate? Ponder, ponder again intensely. The subject can never be exhausted; the more it is studied, the wider will its compass appear. Think what honour you are providing for yourselves, what happiness for others, should you be the happy instrument of converting but one soul to God.

My imagination has sometimes presented me with this picture of a faithful teacher's entrance to the state of her everlasting rest. The agony of dissolution closed, the triumph of faith completed, the conquering spirit hastens to her crown. Upon the confines of the heavenly world, a form divinely fair awaits her arrival. Rapt in astonishment at the dazzling glory of its celestial inhabitant, and as yet a stranger in the world of spirits, she inquires, "Is this Gabriel, chief of all the heavenly hosts, and am I honoured with *his* aid to guide me to the throne of God?" With a smile of ineffable delight, such as gives fresh beauty to an angel's countenance, the mystic form replies, "Dost thou remember little Elizabeth, who was in yonder world a Sunday scholar in thy class? Dost thou recollect the child who wept as thou talkedst to her of sin, and directed her to the cross of the dying Redeemer? God smiled with approbation upon thy effort, and by his own Spirit sealed the impression upon her heart, in characters never to be effaced. Providence removed her from thy care before the fruit of thy labour was visible. The seed however had taken root, and it was the business of another to water what thou didst sow. Cherished by the influence of heaven, the plant of religion flourished in her heart, and shed its fragrance upon her character. Piety, after guarding her from the snares of youth, cheered her amidst the accumulated trials of an afflicted life, supported her amidst the agonies of her last conflict, and elevated her to the mansions of immortality; and now, behold before thee the glorified spirit of that poor child, who under God owes the eternal life on which she has lately entered, to thy faithful labours in the Sunday School, and who is now sent by our Redeemer to introduce thee to the world of glory, as thy first and least reward for guiding the once thoughtless, ignorant, wicked Elizabeth to the world of grace. Hail, happy spirit! Hail, favoured of the Lord! Hail, deliverer of my soul! Hail to the world of eternal glory!"

I can trace the scene no further. I cannot paint the raptures produced in the honoured teacher's bosom by this unexpected interview. I cannot describe the mutual gratitude and love of two such spirits meeting at the entrance of heaven; much less can I follow them to their everlasting mansion, and disclose the bliss which they shall enjoy before the throne of God.

All this, and a thousand times more, is attendant upon the salvation of one single soul. Teachers, what a motive to diligence!

3. *Consider to what indefinite lengths your usefulness may extend.*

Where you design only the improvement of individuals, God, through those individuals, may make you the instruments of blessing multitudes. Where you intend only to produce private worth, God may employ your zeal to form public excellences. You may be the means of cherishing and developing intellectual energies, which will one day be of the greatest benefits to the civil interests of society. And, what is more important, you may be imparting the first rudiments of that knowledge and piety which in their maturity may be employed by God in the service of the sanctuary. Ministers are already preaching to others that Gospel which they themselves first learnt in a Sunday School; and missionaries are winning the remotest tribes with the sweet wonders of that cross which was first displayed to their own view by the efforts of a faithful teacher. Such instances, in all probability, will occur again, and are fairly within the scope of your ambition. In such a case, who can trace the progression of your usefulness, or tell into how wide a stream it will expand as it rolls forward in a course never to be arrested but by the sound of that trumpet which shall proclaim that time shall be no more?

4. Think upon the shortness of the time during which the children can enjoy your care.

In a few, a very few years at most, they will all be gone beyond your instruction. Every Sabbath almost, some are leaving the school, and it is to be feared in many cases retiring beyond the sound of pious admonition for ever. Beyond the age of fifteen or sixteen, few remain to enjoy the privileges of the school; and but few, comparatively, remain so long. Could we even protract the period of childhood, and lengthen the term during which they consider themselves as under our care; could we in every instance be convinced that when they leave our schools they would still continue to enjoy the means of religious culture; even in this case there would be no ground for a relaxation of your diligence; the value of the soul and the importance of its salvation would demand your utmost exertion. But this is not the case. In a year or two you must give them up, and to what? To the violence of their own corruptions, to the strength of their own passions, to the pollution of bad company, without a friend to watch over them, or a single guide to direct them. With the school many of them take leave of the sanctuary; and when they cease to hear the voice of the teacher, listen no more to the joyful sound from the lips of the preacher. What a motive to diligence! Can you be oblivious to its force? Can you read this simple statement and not feel every dormant energy stirring within you? Can you peruse another line and not resolve by the help of God to renew your efforts? Do you not feel the blush of shame for past indifference diffusing itself this moment over your countenance? By all that is dear and invaluable in the eternal interests of the children; by the shortness of the time during which those interests will be under your care; I urge you to be diligent to the very last effort of your soul.

5. Remember how transient is the season during which you can be employed in these labours of love.

If you were certain of reaching the extreme boundaries of human existence, and had the prospect of extending your exertion far into the season of old age; yea, could you ensure an antediluvian life, and employ it all for the good of others; even under these circumstances, you could not be too diligent in the business of your office. Immortality is a theme that will support the weightiest arguments, and justify the most impassioned exhortations. I again repeat it, nor fear the charge of repeating myself, the salvation of immortal souls is the ultimate object of your office; and when professing to labour for such an object, indolence would be inexcusable amidst the range of centuries. But you have not centuries at command. "What is your life? it is even as a vapour, that appeareth for a little while, and then vanisheth away." The uncertainty of life supplies a proverb which we hear every day repeated; and is a fact which we see every day occurring. You may be soon and suddenly called away from the scene of labour. You quit the school every Sabbath without knowing that you will return to it again. Death pays respect neither to youth nor usefulness, but mows down together the tender herb, the fragrant flower, and the noxious weed. The next stroke of his scythe may reach you. Among the names that will be inserted in the report of the present year's proceedings as blotted from the book of mortal life, yours may be read at the next anniversary amidst the sighs and the tears of your fellow-teachers. The place which knows you now may then know you no more for ever. You are labouring in the garden of the Lord; but in the garden are the sepulchres. "Work while it is called today: the night cometh when no man can work. Whatsoever thy hand findeth to do, do it with thy might; for there is no work, nor device, nor knowledge, nor wisdom in the grave, whither thou goest." Enter upon every Sabbath's exertions with the reflection that it may be your last, and be as diligent as if you *knew* that it would be so.

But death is not the only way in which an end can be put to your exertions. In a few years the claims and the cares of a rising family may demand your time at home. For however cordially you may be disposed to continue your benevolent attention to the duties of the school and the interests of the children, the superior demands preferred by a household of your own must be admitted. The honour of doing anything in this way for the cause of God and souls, truth and holiness, may soon be removed beyond your reach. This opportunity will last but a little longer for you to enrich the crown of your rejoicing with fresh gems, or to increase that part of your bliss in heaven which will arise from your witnessing the raptures of those whom you were the instruments of introducing to the mansions of glory. It is a golden season that you now enjoy; it is rapidly passing away; it will never return: diligently improve it therefore while it lasts.

6. *Dwell upon the honour of being instrumental in imparting moral, spiritual, and eternal benefits.*

I have already pointed out, – what indeed requires no proof, – the adaptation of Sunday School instruction to promote the moral excellence of the lower classes; and whoever does this must be acknowledged to be a most useful, and therefore a most honourable, member of the community. The men who have improved and adorned their country by the splendid creations of their genius have had their names emblazoned in the temple of fame, and received all the glory which admiring generations could confer upon their memory. But what is the honour of adorning a city with the finest productions of the chisel or the pencil, and filling it with temples, statues, and paintings, compared with the more useful labour of causing righteousness to flow down its streets like a river, erecting the temples of the Holy Ghost, and raising the children of poverty into the living images of the most High God? In imparting moral and spiritual good, you are conferring benefits which will be perpetuated through infinite ages long after the fashion of this world shall have passed away for ever. This is emphatically to do good. What can equal the renown of being instrumental in reforming, renewing, sanctifying, and adorning the human character; clothing it with the virtues of morality, and investing it with the graces of true godliness? Amongst the ancient Pagans it was a title of the highest honour to be termed, "a benefactor." Hence the apostle argues that for a good man, that is, a man who does good, some would even dare to die. "To love the public," says a wicked writer, who yet found himself compelled to publish this confession, "to study the universal good, and to promote the interest of the world as far as it is in our power, is surely the highest goodness, and constitutes that temper which we call divine." In this consists the true honour of your employment, it is doing good; and to do good is Godlike. God is by no means dependent upon the use of means for the communication of moral and spiritual benefits; he could have accomplished the purposes of His benevolence without the intervention of human instrumentality: this arrangement was expressly intended as a distinguished, though unmerited, favour to the human race.

Dwell upon your character and circumstances, and say if it is not singular goodness in Jehovah to employ *you* in imparting the knowledge of His nature and of His will to your fellow-creatures. The good you do is not merely of a temporal nature; even in this sense it is a high honour to do good. It is noble to feed the hungry, to clothe the naked, to heal the sick, and shelter the aged. The name of the philanthropist shines with a purer, brighter glory on the page of history than any other. If then it be so exalted to do good to the body, how much greater the distinction to relieve the miseries and establish the interests of the immortal spirit; to render our fellow-creatures happy in themselves, and a blessing to others; to fit them for the communion of heaven, after having taught them to be the humble ornaments of society on earth!

To communicate *moral* good is the very noblest employment of an intelligent being. It is that very operation in which the great God takes more delight than in all the rest of his works. This was the object on which the heart of the Redeemer was set when he was made flesh and dwelt among us. For this the Holy Spirit was poured out from above. For this prophets laboured and apostles preached. In the perfect enjoyment of moral benefits will consist the consummation of heaven itself. What a distinguished honour then to be engaged, although in the humblest manner, in such a work! This is to be raised into a likeness of that glorious Being who is good and does good.

A time is fast arriving when it will be seen and felt, that to have been instrumental in conferring spiritual good upon one human soul is a brighter and more lasting glory than the most solid achievements of philosophy, or the most splendid discoveries of science.

Let it be manifest then by your diligence, that you are not unconscious of your privilege. Put not the glory from you. Stir up every energy of your soul to do all the good you can. It is an object worthy of your hallowed ambition. While the warrior is pressing through human misery to pluck his blood-stained laurels, and thinks little of the hazard of his life in the pursuit; while the author by intense study is wasting his strength to gain the prize of literary fame; while the artist is labouring for the applause of futurity: be it your object to do good to the present and eternal interests of your fellow-creatures; and in such a career your ambition is pursuing a loftier flight than all the rest, and ascending into regions to which no mere earthly fame will ever extend.

7. Consider what results might be expected if every teacher were possessed of all suitable qualifications, and were to devote himself to the duties of his office with all possible diligence.

It may be safely affirmed that we have never yet seen, that we have scarcely yet conjectured, the hundredth part of the benefit which the Sunday School system might be made to produce when applied under all the advantages of which it is susceptible. Its adaptation and capacities for improving the condition of the poor are admirable and incalculable. Take the aggregate number of children and teachers at the conjectural statement in the Introduction: then suppose that these myriads of young people to whom the religious education of a million poor children is entrusted were all fully qualified for their office, and all diligently employed in discharging its duties; suppose they were all persons of exemplary piety; possessed of an enlarged acquaintance with the whole range of revealed truth; well instructed in all the general proprieties of human intercourse; endowed with a peculiar aptitude to impart instruction to the youthful mind, and patient in their temper: with such qualifications, suppose they all recognised as the ultimate end of their labours the formation of those truly religious habits in the children which should be connected with the salvation of their immortal souls, and subordinate to this the improvement of their general character, so as to render them kind, gentle, submissive, and orderly: then conceive of these myriads of people thus fitted for their work, devoting themselves to their weekly business of instruction with intense ardour of mind; entering upon the duties of their office, Sabbath after Sabbath, with a deeply interested heart; labouring, with the most affectionate and unwearied care and concern, for their present and eternal welfare; conducting the whole business of instruction with a judicious discrimination of the different tempers they have to deal with; wisely applying all suitable rewards and punishments; punctual and unwearied in their attention; dignified yet affable in their manner; and mingling with all their efforts importunate prayer to Him who alone can render them effectual: in addition to this, suppose them in their behaviour one to another to be universally affectionate, respectful, acting in perfect harmony for the general good, and animated by one mind: suppose, I say, that this were universally the case with the vast body of Sunday School teachers, what results might we not expect? When we consider the adaptation of the system itself to impart religious instruction, and produce religious impression: when we consider that religious education is among God's own instituted means of conversion; when we consider how willing He is to pour out the influence of His Spirit upon the ordinances which he has appointed; especially when we add to this the good effects which have already resulted from the imperfect application of the system; it is scarcely possible to conjecture what a glorious revolution would be visible in the habits of the lower orders of society, if our teachers were universally such as I have described. Instead of hearing occasionally that here and there a child was under religious concern, we should have the pleasing scene before us of great numbers inquiring after the way to Zion, with their faces thitherward. Instead of occasionally witnessing external reformation of conduct in those who were rude, intractable, and violent, we should often receive the gratitude of parents, rendered happy by the moral alteration of their once disobedient and rebellious offspring. The church and the world would both together look to the Sunday School institution as one of the greatest blessings ever bestowed upon man.

But ah! some will say, this is a pleasing vision, a Utopian picture. Why then is it a vision? Why is it Utopian? Only let each teacher resolve, by God's grace, to be all that is here described, (and nothing is described that is impossible,) and then it becomes a glorious reality. Instead of looking at the whole body with a desponding wish that it were indeed entirely what it should be, let each individual look in upon himself, determined that nothing shall be wanting on *his* part to realise this blissful vision. If we would obtain the result which the exertions of all would produce, we must seek it by the contribution of individual diligence.

Amidst the complaints which I have often heard of a lack of success, it has long been my conviction that this lack is to be attributed to the defects of the teachers. Proper views, proper qualifications, and proper diligence in those who have set their hand to the work would be followed with much greater practical effect than it has ever yet been our felicity to witness. The defect is not in the system, but in those who apply it.

Let me then most earnestly enjoin you to seek a larger measure of suitable qualification, and to display still more diligence in this all-important institution; and let your mind be excited to the greatest exertion by a consideration of what would be the result if all teachers discharged their duties with wisdom and assiduity.

8. *Anticipate the approving testimony which at the last day the Lord Jesus will bear to all those who have in any measure promoted his cause.*

That day of righteous retribution, for which all other days were made, is hastening on. Time is drawing to a close; the world is sinking to dissolution; and all mankind converging to "the judgment-seat of Christ, where everyone shall receive the things done in the body according to that he hath done, whether it be good or bad."

Before that tribunal you must render an account of *your conduct*. To that Judge you are amenable both for your personal obedience and the manner in which you discharge your official duties. Then we shall know the real state of your heart, and the true character of your motives. However diligent you may now be in the subordinate duties of your office, yet if not a partaker of real religion, in vain will be the effort to supplement personal defects by official activity, or to turn away the wrath of Him that sits upon the throne with the useless plea, "Lord! Lord! did we not prophesy in thy name?" To be rewarded in that day as a faithful teacher you must first be accepted as a real Christian. Without this you must take your place at the left hand of the Judge, with those whom heaven rejects from her bosom, while hell moves to meet them at their coming. But should you most happily work out your own salvation with fear and trembling, and then labour to glorify God in the salvation of your ignorant charge, not a single effort of your zeal, nor a prayer, nor a word shall be forgotten in that day of righteous reward. First publicly accepted in your person, you will then be as publicly applauded for those services which your humility may now think almost unworthy of His notice, but which His mercy will not suffer Him then to overlook. Then when the deeds of heroes will be passed over in silence, or mentioned with reprobation; when poets, except those who have sung to the harp of piety, and philosophers, except such as have employed their researches to manifest the glory of the First Cause, will sink down without distinction in the general mass; then will the holy useful teacher, attended by the children he had been the means of reclaiming, be presented before the face of an assembled universe, arrayed with infinite honour and glory: not the mighty hosts of Patriarchs and Prophets, Apostles and Evangelists, Reformers and Martyrs, Ministers and Missionaries, pressing to receive their crowns, will throw him into obscurity, or deprive him of his reward; but amidst surrounding millions he will stand single and apart to receive the public plaudits of the Judge: "Inasmuch as you have done it unto the least of these my brethren, you have done it unto me. Well done, good and faithful servant; enter thou into the joy of thy Lord."

Appendix to the Sunday School Teacher's Guide

1 – Musical Performances at Sunday School Anniversaries

IT has of late years become lamentably fashionable to introduce into the service at charity sermons a grand selection of sacred music. In some cases, the vocal performance is attended by a complete instrumental band. Musical effect is as much studied as at an oratorio; and, as in the case of theatrical amusements, the public are lured to the entertainment by a printed bill of the performance. Were a stranger from Rome to pass the doors of our chapels at such a season, he might imagine from the sound of trumpets and kettle-drums, that it was a military mass in some Catholic chapel. I can easily conceive with what force a thinking Papist would say to a Protestant, on such an occasion, "To make this scene complete, you should have painted windows, flowers, embroidered vestments, images, and pictures. For is there more harm in pleasing the eye than the ear?" Now it would be quite bad enough if this profanation of sacred subjects and holy times were confined to the musicians and the congregation; but the children in the Sunday School partake of the mischievous effect, and that in various ways.

1. They are led without realising it to conclude that not *all* entertainment is forbidden even on the Christian Sabbath. For surely it is too much for the credulity of childhood to believe that the performance, as it is generally conducted, is intended for devotion. They thus have their views of the sanctity of the Sabbath considerably lessened. Even in the most quiet

and simple method of conducting the business of an anniversary sermon there is much bustle and disquietude. The children look forward to it for many Sabbaths with feelings of excitement as to a sort of breaking up day. By this means the powerful association which should connect devotion as the purpose of the Sabbath, and moral benefit as the ultimate object of the Sunday School system, is considerably weakened. How much more is this the case when the sermon is attended with all the influence of a grand musical performance!

2. In these cases the best singers among the children are frequently selected to take a share in the performance; some in parts, others in solos. To prepare them for this, much time must be spent in training them. At these exercises, at which no seriousness of mind can be preserved, and which are generally seasons of great entertainment, they are accustomed to treat the most solemn and affecting topics of religion with lightness and irreverence, until their minds grow so over-familiar with them that their hearts become oblivious to all that is awful in their nature and impressive in their influence. It is a most destructive effect when children acquire the habit of treating sacred subjects in a trifling manner, in any way, and on any account. Thus injured by the preparation, their hearts are still more corrupted by the performance. Exhibited to the public, sometimes dressed beyond their station, to please by their appearance and captivate by their melody, they cannot fail to perceive how completely the end of their exhibition is answered. From that hour they lie exposed to all the pernicious influence of pride and vanity. Older, and wiser, and holier minds than are possessed by the children of a Sunday School, have found that admiration has a poisonous effect upon genuine virtue: who then can wonder if the latter amidst the weakness of *their* age and station, feel its deleterious influence? Even the ordinary singing of every Sabbath's worship, where children have been employed in the choir, and exposed to the view of the congregation, has been known, in many instances, to generate a love of display, and a feeling of vanity, exceedingly injurious to their intellectual and moral improvement. How much more on those extraordinary occasions to which I allude! Let children be once led to imbibe the idea that they are taught to sing for entertainment, or any other purpose than as an act of genuine devotion; let them once be led to associate it with the idea of obtaining applause; and they are then in a fair way of seeking to display their vocal powers for the sake of gaining admiration, in company and places very unfriendly to every principle of sound morality and genuine piety.

3. Nor does the mischief end here. The teachers themselves are apt by these means to lose the simplicity of their aim and the spirituality of their

mind. Their attention is drawn off from the spiritual part of the institution, and their ambition directed to making such an exhibition as shall secure applause.

As anniversary sermons however cannot wholly be dispensed with, nor all public exhibition of the children prevented, all that remains for us to do is to be careful that they be attended with as little dissipation and with as much devotion and decorum as possible. But as for the practice of making them occasions for grand musical performances, it is a custom replete with mischief, both to the children and the teachers; a custom which is hastening to corrupt the simplicity of Christian worship, and undermine the sanctity of the Christian Sabbath; a custom which converts the temple of God into a concert-room, and employs the pulpit to hallow, in appearance, the performance. It is quite time for some voice to be raised against the practice, or at least to suggest to the managers of the school, the enquiry, how far it can be justified.

2 – Public Exhibitions of the Children

A PRINCIPLE of just and laudable emulation may be implanted and cherished, without transforming and degrading it into a thirst for admiration, which is almost sure to be the case where the children are called upon to make a display of their talents in public. Praise will ever be found injurious in proportion to these two circumstances; first, the publicity with which it is given; and, secondly, the ignorance of the person on whom it is conferred. If this be correct, the children of a Sunday School should be exposed as little as possible to *public* applause. A love of display is very soon produced, and with great difficulty destroyed. Nor is the mischief confined to those who are the subjects of public distinction. The rest of the children, instead of directing their attention to improvement on its own account, begin to regard it and pursue it only as the road to admiration and distinction. Let either pride or vanity be generally cherished among the labouring classes, and the worst consequences may be expected to accrue to society. The evils which it was once predicted would result from the instruction of the poor, were the mere chimeras of a disordered imagination: not so the fears which arise from injudicious efforts *to force the growth of their understanding, by corrupting the simplicity of their hearts.* No single vice to which the human soul is subject is a more effectual obstacle in the way of his salvation than pride. "How can ye believe," said our glorious Redeemer to the Pharisees, "which receive honour one of another?"

3 – Teaching to Write on the Sabbath

A S this is a controverted point, and the practice is adopted by many who have the spiritual welfare of the children as much at heart as

I possibly can have, I would state my views with the greatest deference, and in the most dispassionate manner, without presuming to condemn those who may happen to differ from me in opinion.

I beg to assume (what I think cannot be denied,) that *moral and religious habits are the ultimate end of Sunday School instruction.* I also take for granted *the sanctity of the Christian Sabbath;* by which I mean, that all works are to be abstained from on that day, but those of devotion, mercy, and absolute necessity.

Try the practice by this test. No one, I suppose, will contend for it as a work of devotion. Is it then a work of necessity? Necessary for what? Not certainly for their moral and religious benefit; for they may be trained up in the fear of God as well without writing as with it. It can just about be classed with the feeblest auxiliaries of virtue or religion. The circumstance of their writing *texts of Scripture* for copies can scarcely be said to render it a moral exercise; since the children think little of the sentiment they are writing, and are almost exclusively intent upon producing a good copy. Everyone knows that nothing is less likely to impress the *heart* than the sentiment written by a child in his copy-book. As to his thus storing his memory with passages of God's Word, it may be observed that the same time which is employed in filling a page with the repetition of one short sentence would be sufficient for him to learn five, and to be made, by a judicious teacher, to comprehend their meaning.

Besides, if the single circumstance of writing texts of Scripture be admitted to justify the practice, would not the same argument allow a girl to work a sampler, provided she wrought upon the canvass a passage of holy writ?

Nor is it absolutely necessary for their *temporal interests;* because the poor may acquire nearly all the advantages and comforts of their station, without being able to write. Not that I think it a superfluous labour to teach the poor to write. Far, very far from it. As a means of improving their worldly condition, I would not only communicate to them this art, but also every kind and every measure of useful knowledge which their circumstances would admit of. The poor cannot possess too much knowledge, provided moral instruction keep pace with it. I cannot yield assent to an opinion so truly unphilosophical, that to improve the understanding is the way to corrupt the heart; I am now only contending that writing is not necessary, either to the spiritual or temporal interests of the poor. Besides, admitting that the art of writing were necessary, still this does not justify the practice of teaching it on the Sabbath, in my opinion, unless it can be proved that it could not be taught them on a weekday. But this cannot be proved, since in many schools where the practice of teaching to write is not admitted on the Sabbath, two or three evenings in the week are devoted to this object, and in such cases people are found sufficiently disinterested to give their time to the work. If it be said, Learning to read is not necessary for the poor, I answer, It is valuable *as a direct and powerful auxiliary to religious and moral improvement.* Let this be proved of writing, and the argument is at an end.

If the practice then be justified at all, it must be defended as *a work of mercy.* But in what light is it a work of mercy? Only as contributing to promote the temporal interests and comfort of the poor. But is this the great design of the Sabbath to assist the poor in promoting their temporal interests? If so, may we not teach them many other things which, although generally considered unlawful, would strictly accord with this principle, and carry it on to much greater perfection? We might teach boys accounts and book-keeping; for this would be of great service to them. To boys in manufacturing towns we might impart the rudiments of mechanics; to those who are intended for carpenters, painters, glaziers, etc, we might teach the principles of mensuration; and the youth of seaport towns we might instruct in navigation. Especially, on this principle must it be lawful to teach girls to sew and knit, since these acquisitions are far more necessary qualifications for the female head of a poor man's family, than writing is to either of the parents. This remark applies with double force to manufacturing towns, where female children are in general put out to work long before they have acquired these valuable qualifications of a poor man's wife. I confess I do not see how the force of this reasoning is to be avoided.

The objection to the practice may be generally stated thus. *It is appropriating the Sabbath to a purpose for which it was never intended, without a sufficient reason to justify such a misapplication of the holy day.*

The evils resulting from the practice appear to me to be many and great.

1. It is injurious to the minds of the teachers, by secularising the Sabbath, and increasing the danger of their losing the enjoyment of its religious ordinances. The circumstances necessarily attendant upon the business of teaching one or two hundred children to write, must have a powerful tendency, I should think, to distract the mind, and not only divert it from all devotional subjects for the time, but to unfit it for them when they are speedily to follow. The mending of pens, the examination of copies, the correction of mistakes, seem to me likely to exert a most unfavourable influence upon a devotional frame of mind. It is also very likely to sink a teacher's view and aim from the ultimate end of his labours to what is only inferior and subordinate.

2. I think it injurious to the minds and habits of the children. It must have a tendency to take off their minds from the chief design of their being

instructed. It is of vast importance to their religious improvement that they should clearly perceive that this is with us the purpose for which we collect them together. They should be convinced, not merely by being told, but by all they see in the business of the school, that they are assembled not only to be taught to read and write, but to be made holy and happy. This would fix their eye where ours ought to be directed, and prepare them to be co-workers with us in the business of their salvation. Now the act of teaching them to write must, I think, have a tendency to lower their aim, as well as that of their teachers, and lead them to attach less importance to moral impression.

Besides, has not the practice the effect of destroying the seriousness of that religious instruction which, in many schools, is still carried on in other parts of their mode of education? Do the children and their teachers come from the writing-desk either to the solemnities of public worship, or the more private exhortations of the schoolroom, with the same degree of preparedness as they otherwise would do? Is not the awe, which should ever attend the spirit to the means of religious instruction, gone?

3. A still more serious mischief is, in my judgement, likely to arise from the practice: *it has a tendency to undermine the sanctity of the Sabbath in the opinion of the children.* Those who live in large towns have ample opportunity of knowing how awfully the Sabbath is neglected and profaned by the labouring classes. Whole streets are to be found where the men are to be seen loitering about in indolence, and the women busily engaged in domestic affairs. Sabbath-breaking is peculiarly one of the vices of the poor, and it is the parent of many others. Scarcely a felon is carried from the bar of justice to the hulks or the gallows, but confesses that his career of iniquity commenced with this crime. Everything should be done to *raise,* in the estimation of the poor, the sanctity of the Sabbath, and to bind its obligations more closely on the conscience. If it were possible to err on the side of over-strictness, our leaning should be decidedly to this. While a reverence for the Sabbath remains, all veneration for the *God* of the Sabbath cannot be entirely lost. It is the last spark of moral sense which lingers upon the horizon of a sinner's mind, before he is overtaken by the midnight darkness of a blinded conscience, and hurried away by his own furious lusts, or swept from the precipice of infidelity into the bottomless pit which yawns beneath. Everything then should be done to create in the minds of the young a habitual and scrupulous dread of the least infraction upon the solemnity of this holy day. Whether this is most effectually done by teaching them to write on the Sabbath let impartial judges decide. Accustomed to this practice at the school, who can wonder if afterwards they should feel little hesitation to

write letters or keep whatever accounts may be necessary in the circumstances of their humble history?

Perhaps it will be replied, that there is the same objection against teaching to read as to write on the Sabbath, that it secularises the day, and impairs the strength of its devotional obligations. This is not just. Learning to read *is a direct and obvious means of moral and religious benefit;* and the connection is so close, that a child of the least discernment perceives it without being reminded of it. The very books in which he learns the art are the Old and New Testaments; so that at the very time he is acquiring his ability to read, he is imbibing the principles of divine truth and genuine godliness. These, or else extracts taken from them, or hymns founded upon their contents, are all they ever read within the precincts of the school. Every child may be easily made, and should be made, to perceive that learning to read has a close connection with his spiritual and eternal interests; and that which the mind habitually associates with religious improvement is never likely to become a means of undermining in its feelings the sanctity of that day which we are enjoined by awful sanctions to remember and to hallow.

4 – Savings' Banks for Children

THE scheme which has been lately recommended to the public, denominated "the savings' bank," as a depository for the small sums which the labouring classes can spare from their weekly support, is adopted in many schools with considerable benefit. Except during calamitous times, the children, especially in manufacturing districts, spend many a penny and twopence on the most useless trash. To prevent this waste of money, they are encouraged to bring every halfpenny that is not required for their present support, and deposit it in the hands of the superintendent, or some other person, who keeps an account open with every child who has deposited anything.

This money they are of course allowed to draw out whenever they want it; this however should never be done but at the desire of their parents, in order that it may not be improperly applied. In some cases a premium is allowed; which indeed should be always adopted when the funds of the school will allow it. It is the least advantage of this plan, that it saves for the benefit of the children a considerable sum of money, which would otherwise be spent in useless gratifications of their appetites. There is a still greater benefit likely to accrue. It teaches them from their childhood *habits of economy and frugality.* Those who have had much to do with the poor know and lament how deplorably wanting they are in such habits. They are the most improvident of their species, scarcely ever looking beyond the present, wasteful of *the much*, and regardless of *the little*. Greater sums are often squandered, because they are great; and little sums not saved, because they are little. They are sadly defective in that policy which takes care of the shilling, and leaves the pound to take care of itself. Hence the greatest profusion is often followed in their families by the greatest scarcity, since, even in the best of times, and by the best of workmen, there is seldom any provision made against a season of sickness or necessity. Much of the distress which prevails during a stagnation of trade, or a time of domestic affliction, may be traced up to this wretched want of economy and foresight. We cannot then confer upon a poor man a greater earthly benefit in his station, than a habit of frugality. If this be ever done with effect, it must be accomplished while he is young; and a more effectual method can scarcely be devised than the plan I now recommend. Let the children be taught that every farthing spent in trash is lost, and be encouraged to bring all they can spare to the savings' fund. At the end of the year, or any stated period, let them be carefully impressed with the idea, that a considerable sum, by the increase of a little self-denial, has been collected from what at the time seemed scarcely worth saving. Let them, when the money is in their hands, and their hearts leaping at the sight, be impressively taught, by an appeal to their own experience, the important sentiment that much is made up of *many littles*. Let them be very forcibly reminded of the ultimate benefits arising from preferring future good to present gratification. We are thus communicating, in an almost imperceptible manner, those saving and frugal habits which will be of service to them all the days of their life. We are doing more than this; for we are actually communicating moral benefit. Everything that induces a human mind to forego immediate gratification for distant good; everything that makes the future predominate over the present; everything, in short, which makes a man live by faith and hope, seems to be a preparation for that temper which displays itself by "looking not at the things which are seen and temporal, but at the things which are unseen and eternal."

And even where no direct moral good is produced, it will ever be found that a saving and frugal temper is connected with a spirit of proper and praiseworthy independence. So that we are by this means raising a barrier against the swelling tide of national embarrassment, which is flowing in continually upon us from the nature and influence of the poor laws.

This view of things justifies the remarks which are contained in the preface of this work, concerning the importance of the Sunday School system, as throwing into our hands the whole labouring population of the kingdom, to form their minds and manners in what way we please. And if we may judge from the present state of things, this is an advantage which should be eagerly seized by every friend of his country, as well as every friend of religion.

5 – *The Results of Sunday School Teaching*

SOME people have frequently experienced considerable discouragement in this great and good work, by not seeing more visible benefit result to the lower classes of society from these efforts. I have said much already on this head; I beg leave, however, in addition to remark, that there are two ways by which to judge of the benefit resulting from this mode of education. The first is by considering the good communicated, and, secondly the evil prevented. On the first I have already had occasion to dwell. This is incalculable and inconceivable. I shall, however, make a few remarks upon the second criterion, the evil prevented. Now, admitting all that can be said about the present profligacy of multitudes of the labouring classes and the alarming increase of juvenile delinquency which has been discovered during the last twenty years, still let us take into the account the evil that has been prevented.

It should be recollected, that since the Sunday School system has been in operation, the commerce of this country has swelled to unparalleled greatness. This has been attended of course with a proportionate increase of population. It is not, perhaps, saying too much, if we affirm that the labouring classes, in most manufacturing districts, have almost trebled in number since Robert Raikes commenced his exertions at Gloucester. Let it be conceived then what might have been the state of things now, if these accumulated masses of the population had been left as an intellectual chaos for the spirit of mischief to brood upon amidst the clouds of ignorance. The period now alluded to has been a season of uncommon peril to the national morals. *Infidelity* at one time made desperate efforts to corrupt the public mind, not only of the higher, but also of the lower, classes of society. Paine's writings were especially addressed to the passions and prejudices of the multitude. During the greater part of this period the lower classes of society have also been exposed to the demoralising influence of a state of warfare. *The military system*, which has been adopted to such an unprecedented extent in the annals of British history, has had a negative influence upon the morals of the poor. It must also be admitted, that while they have thus had an opportunity of trying their physical strength, *very many efforts have been employed at different times to inflame their passions against one party or other in the troubled regions of politics*. Their just importance in the body politic was never so well known before, nor were they ever before in such danger of abusing it. To all this must be added the *impossibility*, if they were generally so disposed, *of their gaining access to the solemnities of public worship*, on account of the disproportion between the population and the temples of religion. Now, let all these things be taken into the account. Let it be remembered what increased opportunities have been afforded for their corrupting and being corrupted; let it also be recollected what principles of corruption have actually been at work; and then it will be evident that it can be ascribed only to the gradual diffusion of moral principle by the means of Sunday Schools that these mischiefs have been counteracted, and the labouring classes restrained in any degree within the bounds of sub-ordination and order. When, therefore, we look at them as they are, and lament how little real good has been done, let us, at the same time, rejoice to contemplate how much evil has been prevented.

A Memoir of Elizabeth Bales
A Pattern for Sunday School Teachers and Tract Distributors

"Who hath despised the day of small things?"

"In the obscurity of retirement," says a striking modern writer, "amid the squalid poverty and revolting privations of a cottage, has often been my lot to witness scenes of magnanimity and self-denial, as much beyond the belief as the practice of the great; a heroism borrowing no support, either from the gaze of the many or the admiration of the few, yet flourishing amidst ruins and on the confines of the grave; a spectacle as stupendous in the moral world as the falls of the Missouri in the natural; and like that mighty cataract doomed to display its grandeur only where there are no eyes to appreciate its magnificence."

ALTHOUGH this striking paragraph is not altogether descriptive of the subject of the present memoir, yet it occurred to my mind in connection with the humble lot and beautiful history of Elizabeth Bales.

Elizabeth Bales was born at Nottingham, of parents who though once in tolerably respectable circumstances, – her father being by trade a hosier, – were gradually losing their standing in life, and declining in their means of comfortable support. Mr Bales, with the hope of retrieving his affairs, determined to remove to Ireland. On their approaching the shore of that country a violent storm arose which drove them back to the coast of Wales, where the vessel struck upon the sands, and they were in imminent peril of shipwreck. The passengers were lowered by ropes into a boat, in order to be taken ashore from the vessel: among them was Elizabeth, the subject of this memoir, then about four years old, who up to that time had been a healthy and well-formed child. It is conjectured that in the act of lowering her into the boat she received some spinal injury, for from that time she complained much of her back, which soon after exhibited early signs of deformity. This continued to increase until she presented an affecting spectacle of bodily infirmity. Through the days of youth she was a most dutiful and affectionate daughter, and possessed considerable sweetness of temper and placidity of disposition. From a very early period she manifested a general reverence for religion, and a vague notion of its importance. As a child she used to assemble her little companions, when she would read to them the Scriptures, and sing and pray with them; but it was not until she was about seventeen years of age that she had any clear and impressive sense of her own fallen and sinful condition, or of the way of pardon and eternal life through faith in our Lord Jesus Christ. She was then residing at Hanwell, near London, where she heard the preaching of Mr Gregory, who kept a large boarding school, and preached in his own house. Here she was much loved, and received great attention on account of her engaging manners, sweetness of temper, and piety.

Her father, having lost his all by the failure of his trade, removed with his family to this town, where he earned a scanty livelihood by weaving cotton gloves upon a stocking loom which he kept in his house, and selling them as opportunity presented. In consequence of her deformity, Elizabeth could not be put to any bodily labour, and therefore employed herself in sewing the seams of the gloves which were woven by her father. Poverty at length in most of its privations and rigours, took possession of the dwelling of this gradually sinking family, who still however contrived to do without the parochial allowance.

By the labours of a few pious and zealous young people connected with my congregation a Sunday School was set up in that part of the town where Elizabeth lived. In addition to the instructions delivered in the school, preaching was carried on in the room where the children met. The neighbourhood of Great Barr Street and Garrison Lane, where these operations were conducted, peculiarly needed such efforts as, from more causes than one, morals were at that time in a very low state in that locality, and there were no places of religious worship within even a moderate distance. Among those who listened to the glad tidings of salvation was the subject of these pages. Her views of religion here became still more clear, and as a sinner condemned by the law, she believed in Christ, the great subject of the gospel testimony, enjoyed peace through faith, and became altogether a new creature. Evangelical piety not only made her happy, but excited in her heart a wish to be useful in leading others to that Saviour whom she had found to her unutterable consolation; and she sought to be admitted as a teacher in the Sunday School. Her personal appearance rendered her rather ineligible, and made it somewhat doubtful whether it was desirable to expose her to derision and contempt; but her earnestness, combined with great simplicity and modesty, overcame this objection, and she took her place among her young charge. The school was at that time held in an inconvenient upper room, to which the only access was by a kind of step ladder; and oftentimes, when in a state of greater weakness than usual, it was necessary for one of the stronger teachers to carry this good girl in his arms up the steep ascent, and deposit her in the scene of her Sabbath occupations.

In the year 1824, Elizabeth entered into the fellowship of the church under my care, when a written testimony was borne to her character and conduct by the deacon who visited her at the time of her admission to our communion, from which the following is an extract:

"Elizabeth Bales first became acquainted with us in consequence of her desire to be made useful as a teacher, in our Bordesley Sunday School; having expressed that wish to a pious woman, well known in that neighbourhood, it was made known to us, and she was introduced there about a year ago. Her conduct as a teacher during the whole of that time has been one unvaried, beautiful exhibition of what a teacher's conduct ought always to be, the most exact regularity, and an assiduous and unwearied attention to each and every child in her class: but in order to put the full value upon these good qualities, it should be known that her health is so delicate as would furnish a sufficient apology for altogether declining the employment, and her appearance such as must awaken the painful sympathy of the benevolent spectator; and yet she commands the respect of her infant charge, and well maintains her gentle authority amongst them; and although they are at that early age when it is so difficult to fix the attention, the mild and unremitting efforts of their instructress have produced a change too obvious to be overlooked in comparison with less favoured classes. Conduct like this could not fail to attract the esteem of those who observed it, the marks of its heavenly origin could hardly be mistaken; the superintendent of the school therefore felt it his duty to invite her to be united with us in closer ties. After due deliberation and obtaining permission from her parents, she at length consented."

From this extract it will be seen with what efficiency, notwithstanding her personal appearance, Elizabeth discharged her duties as a Sunday School teacher. Her deformity was greater than is usually found in those who are affected with spinal distortion; and when we consider how frequently this is an object of ridicule or disgust with children who have not been trained to restrain their feelings by the courtesies of society, we can imagine that there must have been some latent and counteracting power to awe the rude spirits of her young charge. This lay in her eminent piety, in the sweetness and placidity of her temper, in her judicious affection for the children, and in her constant punctuality in the discharge of her duties, in addition to which, it may be added, she possessed a soft musical voice, and a rather engaging countenance.

Never did a teacher enter more fully, or more delightfully into the occupations of her important office, or more clearly understand and more steadily pursue its ultimate end. Her eye was fixed on the souls of the children; her heart longed for their salvation; and her efforts were unwearied to engage their affections for Christ. To teach them to read, though she was assiduous in this, was the lowest of her aims; her great object was to form their religious character. Not content with teaching them on the Sabbath day, she would meet them at other times for instruction, conversation, and prayer: nor were they reluctant to comply with her wishes, or to gather round her chair, to listen to the heartfelt expressions of her concern for their spiritual welfare: yet, from her poverty, she had nothing else to give them but the love of a heart devoted to their welfare. The intelligent and observant stranger would have been struck to notice the almost reverent and affectionate attention with which a circle of poor girls would look up to that little deformed creature that took her seat in the midst of them as their instructress: and her influence over them was another demonstration of the power as well as the excellence of goodness. This was acquired in part, as I have just hinted, by the interest she took in her children's concerns out of the school. She did not lay aside her labours when she left the school, never to take them up again until the next Sabbath morning, but carried them through the week, by enquiries after the absentees, and by visiting and praying with those who were sick. It was a stimulus to regularity of attendance on the part of the children to know that the absentees would be sought after by their vigilant teacher; and it was a comfort to those in trouble to be assured with equal certainty that their sorrows would come under the notice of her attentive eye, and the sympathy of her feeling heart. All this, of course, tended to produce, and did produce, for her the gratitude and respect of the children's parents.

From the time that Elizabeth's own heart was renewed by the grace of God, she showed that true and necessary evidence of personal religion, a deep concern for the salvation of others, and especially for those who dwelt in her own neighbourhood, where it must be admitted she witnessed the aboundings of iniquity, and the overflowings of ungodliness. She was not unconcerned about the conversion of the distant heathen, but the state of the heathen around her still more deeply affected her heart. She felt all the claims of locality: this was perhaps the predominant feeling of her heart, and trait of her character; she seemed to feel that each Christian should be a light in his own vicinity, especially when, as was the case with hers, that neighbourhood is characterised by peculiar darkness and depravity. Her heart groaned over the wickedness of the people, and like Lot, she vexed her righteous soul daily, because of the filthy conversation of the wicked, – the immortal souls perishing at her own door, – and was stirred up to seek their salvation.

To aid the good work of reformation which the church, of which she was so consistent a member, were attempting in her vicinity, by various means, and among the rest by a religious tract society, Elizabeth commenced the labours of a tract distributor. In this new office she was no less diligent, devoted, and affectionate, than in that of a Sunday School teacher. In winter and in summer, amidst storm and calm, when the sun was blazing with summer heat, and the winter's snow was deep upon the ground, this indefatigable little creature would be seen pursuing her rounds, and going from house to house upon her visits of mercy to the dark souls of those who inhabited them, and when permitted, as was very common, she would read and explain the tracts which she brought to them. Sometimes she would be refused admittance by the surly growl of brutish ignorance and profanity, and at others would be distressed by the scornful sneer of infidelity, with which the neighbourhood was much infested: but nothing daunted, she would mildly continue, and usually won an entrance for her tract by the gentleness of her manner, and the unruffled serenity of her spirit. It may be imagined that even in her presence, – contemptible as it might seem to have been, – many an athletic form of impiety stood abashed, like Satan before Ithuriel, and felt how awful goodness is. For this she prepared and armed herself by fervent prayer. Before setting out on her rounds she would say to the associate of her labours, "Come, my dear, let us look up to God for His help and blessing:" and then in a strain of sweet and fervent supplication invoke the grace of Him, without whom nothing is wise, good, or strong.

Insult or derision however was the exception, not the rule. She was generally regarded in her neighbourhood with something approaching reverence, which eminent and consistent piety, united with extraordinary benevolence, alone could inspire. Sturdy and powerful men would say to her, "If anyone should dare to molest or hinder thee in the discharge of thy business, send for us, and we will always fight for thee." To which she would reply with a grateful smile, "I can best fight for myself." Meaning, by her gentleness, and dependence upon God, which would disarm all hostility, and be her best protection. Her usual reception was that of great respect and kindness; nor was it uncommon to hear the exclamation, as she approached, "Here comes our little angel: bless her."

The labour of tract distributing made her personally acquainted with the sorrows of her poor neighbours, arising from penury and disease. She had an ear for every tale of woe, and became a visitor of the sick, to whom the kindness of her manner much endeared her; and who frequently sent for "the little woman," as they called her, though, as in the case of her Sunday School children, they could expect no money from her, to read and talk to them, and pray with them. These requests, when able to comply with them, she never refused; and she was welcomed as a ministering angel to many a wretched abode, where the glad tidings of salvation were listened to with deep and solemn attention, as they fell in the soft tones of her sweet voice upon the sufferer's ear. Having an excellent gift, as well as much of the grace, of extempore prayer, her impressive and beseeching supplications were as much valued as her instructive counsels, and perhaps more. These visits were of course usually, though not always, paid to persons of her own sex. In this way she may be said to have almost acted the part of a town missionary. Her labours in this department of Christian activity were incessant and laborious, and they were carried on under the pressure of almost constant, and frequently severe pain. Sometimes she would come in, sit down, and faint, and after recovering from her exhaustion, would set off again upon a visit to some other object of her pious concern. It was a frequent occurrence for her not to return from her ministrations in the sick chamber until ten o'clock, and then to receive another summons to the sick or dying bed of some afflicted and anxious neighbour, who coveted the wisdom of her instructions, and the efficacy of her prayers. The clock has struck twelve sometimes before she has returned to her own dwelling, when upon being expostulated with the next day by her mother, regarding the injury she must do herself by such efforts, she would reply, "I must work while I can, for I may not be able to work long:" and it was a common exclamation, "I cannot do work enough for Christ." Her mother has often gone into her room and found she had fainted upon the floor.

It is not to be wondered at that by such conduct as this, Elizabeth had acquired such a character for sanctity and benevolence, that her neighbours were ashamed or afraid to sin in her presence. The swearer would not like to utter his oath if she were by, licentious levity would grow serious if she were coming, and the Sabbath breakers, when going to purchase articles on the holy day at the shop in her vicinity, would feel a pang of conscience as they passed her door, and look up at her window to see if her reproving eye was upon them; and if this were the case, went home with a tolerable certainty of an expostulatory visit or note next day.

I introduce here one specimen of her tract visits, with its results. She was making her visits one day in company with her most intimate friend, Mary Cox, the sister of an excellent Wesleyan Missionary in Africa, when a woman asked them to go in and visit her son, then dangerously ill. The history of this youth was somewhat affecting. A caravan of wild beasts happening to be in town, he most imprudently climbed up the back of one of the waggons, and put his arm through an air hole into the den of a tiger, when the beast instantly sprung at the arm and bit it clean off in a moment. He was carried to the hospital, where a cure was effected. Soon afterwards he was again carried to the same public institution with a white swelling in one of his knees, which rendered an amputation of the leg necessary. This was not the end of the poor youth's misery, for no long time elapsed before the other knee became affected, and mutilated as he was, there appeared no other means of saving life, but by amputating the other limb. This he refused to undergo, preferring to die rather than to endure further torture and mutilation. While lying in this hopeless condition, Elizabeth visited him, and found him in some concern about the state of his soul. She poured into his ear the glad tidings of salvation, and soothed his troubled spirit with the hope of mercy through faith in Christ. He listened with deep attention, expressed his gratitude for her visit, and begged a repetition of it. She lost no time in making her friend Mr Derrington, then employed as the town missionary for the neighbourhood, acquainted with the case, who immediately visited the youth, and paid him great attention. His mind was opened by the Lord to receive the truth, and having believed the gospel, was brought to the enjoyment of great peace. Elizabeth continued also to visit him, and contributed to his growth in knowledge and grace. As a proof of the state of his mind, both in holiness and happiness, the following incident might be mentioned. His father was one day drinking and singing, in the yard just under his window. To drown the voice of noisy merriment, he commenced a song of his own, which he had learnt, one of the songs of Zion, that simple little hymn:

> "Mark the righteous man, and see
>   Peace and joy his steps attend;
> All his path is purity;
>   Happy is his end.
>
> "Come and see his dying bed;
>   Peacefully his moments roll;
> Angels hover round his head;
>   Heav'n receives his soul.
>
> "Come and view his mortal grave;
>   Silence and repose are there;
> Never more shall sorrow's wave
>   Wreck the slumberer."

O, there is something at once touching and beautiful in the idea of this dying youth turning the subject of his own mortality into song, and making his "dying bed," and "mortal grave," the very theme with which to drown the sound of the drunkards' voices. At length he prevailed upon the party to break up, sent for his father into his room, and sang over to him the hymn with which he had been entertaining his holy mind during the scene of conviviality. After lingering awhile on the borders of the grave with a most joyful hope of immortality, he laid down his mutilated body in the grave, to await the perfection of the resurrection, while his spirit departed to be with Christ, leaving Elizabeth and her female companion to rejoice in the blessed fruit of their tract labours. Mr Derrington addressed a large congregation on the following Sabbath after the burial, and it may be hoped not without spiritual effect upon many minds.

After carrying on for some time the Sunday School and the preaching, in the inconvenient room already alluded to, the congregation in Carrs Lane erected, at a cost of about four hundred pounds, a new building in the same neighbourhood, which like the other was also to serve the double purpose of chapel and school house. This was a matter of great delight to Elizabeth on many accounts. On many occasions she would borrow the keys and retire there, either for more leisure and a better opportunity for meditation and prayer than she could always command at home; or else to pour out her heart to God in fervent supplication for His Spirit to descend on the labours which were carried on upon that, to her, most consecrated spot: and who shall say, or who can conceive, what communings with God were maintained in those seasons of seclusion, by her wrestling spirit; or how much of the success of the efforts pursued there, both by teacher and preachers, is to be traced up to her solitary intercessions in the place where they were made.

In that building Elizabeth was a constant attendant, year after year, upon the ordinances of public worship, as often as the doors were opened, on weekdays, as well as on the Sabbaths; and in all weathers, on winter evenings as well as summer mornings. She was exceedingly fond of the prayer meetings, and as long as her health permitted, was always present at the one which was held at the chapel early on Sunday morning, though to accomplish this she had to rise as early as five o'clock, in order to recover her breath from the fatigue of dressing, and have time for her own private devotions. It was her custom by a rapid glance round the congregation, to ascertain who among the habitual worshippers were absent from the house of God, and then to call upon them, either on her way to chapel in the evening, or next day; not however to arraign, accuse, and scold, but in some such gentle language as this, to expostulate; "My dear, I did not see you at chapel this afternoon." In all her labours, whether as teacher in the Sunday School, as a tract distributor, or a visitor of the sick, her great and constant object was to get the people to attend the preaching of the gospel, knowing as she well did, "that faith cometh by hearing, and hearing by the word of God." Nor can anyone engage in any way of usefulness more easy, or more likely to be effectual, than in persuading those who neglect the means of grace, to attend constantly upon the preaching of the gospel. Thousands have been thus the means of winning souls to Christ, and saving them from death; and thousands more, not excepting the youngest, or the weakest, may be blessed in the same manner if they would try.

Some few years ago the Christian community at Carrs Lane, considering that the end for which Christian churches are set up is to sound out the word of the Lord all around them, established and supported by the subscriptions of its own members a town mission. One of the first spheres of its operation was that part of the vicinity of Birmingham in which their chapel was built, and in which Elizabeth lived: the exact locality being called Garrison Lane. In the same neighbourhood lived Mr Derrington, already mentioned, one of her fellow-members, who had made himself exceedingly useful in visiting the sick, instructing the ignorant, and preaching in turn with others at the chapel, and from whom she had received the kindest and most humane attention. Her gratitude to him was exceedingly ardent, and it was her earnest hope that he would be appointed as the town missionary for that neighbourhood. Her desire for this arose in part from a high opinion of his adaptation to the situation, and an anxious hope that he would be a blessing to her poor neighbours; and in part also from Christian regard to one, whose instructions and sympathy had contributed so much to her growth in knowledge, grace, and religious enjoyment.

Nor was he alone in his kindness. Her pastor felt it a duty and a pleasure to go to her lowly cot and her sick chamber, though prevented by his numerous other commitments, large church, and distance from her locality, from seeing her as often as he otherwise would have done: and he knew moreover that she lived amidst a circle of friends, all of whom, for the love and reverence they bore for her, delighted to flock around her, until she was in danger of being oppressed by the attentions of Christian friendship.

It should be here stated, that for several of the last years of her life, Elizabeth, through the increasing poverty of her father, who could scarcely earn the means of subsistence for himself and his aged wife, was supported in great measure by the bounty of the church of which she was a member; in the dispensing of which, the deacons felt it a pleasure to be more than ordinarily liberal in administering to her wants: this resource, and the kindness of friends, supplied her not only with necessaries, but the comforts of life, and it may be hoped that she was thus rather a help than a burden to her impoverished parents.

I now mention a peculiar circumstance in her history, not for the purpose of exciting wonder, as if there were anything unprecedented, much less supernatural, in it, but as being a part of her history, and a part which excited no little talk at the time of its occurrence, and demonstrated the general tenor of her mind and heart. About three years ago she was liable to extraordinary fits of unconsciousness, or diseased sleep, from which nothing could rouse her, neither noises, pungent aromatics applied to the nostrils, nor bodily agitation; and during which, she would go through, in an audible voice, various soliloquies, religious exercises, and conversations. Take for example the following, which was the first that occurred in the presence and hearing of Mr Derrington, though he heard many afterwards. Supposing herself making her round of visits to the dwellings of her neighbours, she comes, in imagination, to the house of a poor aged female. Seating herself near the object of her anxiety, she addressed her as follows:

"Come, old woman, I am called to see you; do you think anything about your soul? You are getting old, and if you don't think about your soul, it will soon be too late, and there is no change in the grave; but we must be changed. Reach me that book; here is a beautiful hymn, we sometimes sing it at chapel;

"'Come we that love the Lord.'

"Do you love the Lord? If you do not, you cannot sing that hymn: I do love the Lord. The hymn is a long one; the verse I think is:

"'Then let our songs abound,
    And every tear be dry,
We're marching thro' Immanuel's ground
    To fairer worlds on high.'

"Yes marching, I have been marching a long time; I don't mean marching as soldiers march, but marching to heaven. I have had many storms and conflicts by the way, but I would not go back; no, there is a sweetness in it. But what makes it sweet, do you know? It is because Christ is with me. There is a passage in Scripture which says, 'Come unto me all ye that labour and are heavy laden, and I will give you rest,' rest, rest; rest for what? The soul rests from what? Sin. Oh how sweet that rest is; I wish all the people were weary of sin. The Scriptures say, 'The wages of sin is death;' what poor wages: we cannot live by them; I cannot live by them, and yet how many are serving Satan. And then how sweet the other part of the passage: 'The gift of God is eternal life.' Is not that beautiful? You don't know much about it, because you don't go to chapel. There is a verse in a hymn which begins,

"'How firm a foundation, ye saints of the Lord;'

"Yes, it is a firm foundation, it is one that will stand: men build, but their foundations will not stand in the day of trial. I build upon Christ, and that is a good foundation; I have nothing to build upon of my own; my works are very imperfect. Then the last verse but one of that hymn:

"'The flame shall not hurt thee; I only design
Thy dross to consume, thy gold to refine.'

"Here afflictions are compared to fire; you know fire is sharp, and so is affliction. But God says, I only design thy dross to consume. I don't mean the dross of metals, gold or iron: my brother works at iron and there is a great deal of rust upon it, but I don't mean that; it is the dross of sin; I have a great deal of dross. In the last verse it says,

"'I'll never, no, never; no, never forsake.'

Father, mother, brother, sister, husband, wife, may forsake, but Christ will not, and that's my Saviour, who will not forsake me. Well I must go to chapel now, but I will come again; I will ask Mr D___ to call and see you, perhaps he may be the means of saving your soul."

Being anxious to be present at one of her seasons of mental exclusion and isolation from the world around her, I called one day, with the hope that it would take place while I was there. My wish was gratified. I took my seat by her bedside. For a while her lips moved with great rapidity, as if in conversation, but without perceivable sound. At length she said, "Let us sing the following hymn:

"Alas! and did my Saviour bleed."

Here she paused, and described the time, place, and circumstances of her first hearing this pathetic strain, and the effect it produced upon her mind. She then applied the sentiment of the hymn to herself, in a most simple yet impressive manner, "Died for me, died for poor Betsy." After many remarks of this kind, expressive of her wonder that grace should be bestowed upon her, she broke forth into a song, in a sweet, clear, musical voice, and in a tune which, I think, was composed on the occasion, as I had no acquaintance with it whatever. Verse after verse followed in the same tune, and with a soliloquy on each. She then gave out this text; "That no man take thy crown." She described with great correctness the nature of the crown, stating that it was not a golden one, such as monarchs wear, but a crown of life and glory that fadeth not away: she then considered the people who were invited to possess the crown; and again thought of herself, saying, "There is a crown for poor Betsy, and a crown for my dear father and mother, if they will have one." Next came the enemies who want to take from us our crown, especially Satan, whose power she described as being limited, though very great. It certainly was no contemptible sermon. But the most impressive part of the scene was the prayer which followed. It occupied between seven and ten minutes, without a single pause, incoherence, or word out of place. Among other subjects she remembered with respectful affection her pastor, then seated, though unknown to her, by her bedside; nor did she forget one dear to him, since risen above the need of prayer: but still the burden of her supplication was Mr Derrington and Garrison Lane; for whom, as was natural, the most fervent aspirations of her heart rose to heaven. It must have been an eye more unused to weep than mine is, that could refrain from shedding tears, while listening to this slumbering wrestler with God, pouring out from the inner and hidden world of her own thoughts, such affecting petitions for my happiness and usefulness. I am not the only individual who wept over that scene; a physician whom I know, and who often visited her chamber, has been seen profusely shedding tears as he listened to the unconscious strains of her prayer or praise. Now I do not mean for a moment to insinuate that there was anything of vision or trance in all this; it was an unconscious action of the brain, which continued more or less, at times, for some months; but, as the terrors and remorse of the slumbering sinner show the state of his heart and conscience, so did these exercises of Elizabeth's soul, when the judgement and will were suspended, and the heart was left to follow its own unchecked and unguided impulses, show what objects held her soul in the spell of their fascination. It should be observed here, that on a return to consciousness she remembered nothing that had passed through her mind during the fit.

Advancing infirmity had now confined Elizabeth to her sick chamber. But could the energies of her zeal be repressed? Could she cease to be useful? No. But what could she do? They whose hearts are bent on doing good, will find means of usefulness everywhere and at all times, not excepting even the bed of disease and the confines of the grave. This devoted teacher could no longer go to her class of Sunday scholars, but her class could come to her. A sick chamber has few attractions for a set of lively girls; yet in this case they gladly obeyed the summons, and occasionally hastened to the retreat of their beloved instructress. Solemn, serious, and affectionate was the manner in which she there taught and counselled them, and commended them to God in prayer. Nor was this the extent of her efforts to do good: from her seclusion she sent forth many letters to her friends, the writing of which must have put her to severe pain.

The influence of Elizabeth among the young females who attended the chapel, or taught in the Sunday School, was of the happiest kind; her good sense, and affectionate disposition, united with her eminent piety and well-known zeal, secured at once their esteem and regard. They made her their friend in the various troubles of a spiritual nature which agitated their minds; and they laid open the secrets of their hearts with a freedom which they could not use towards another; and often have they returned from her chamber, relieved from doubts, fears and perplexities, with which they entered it. By them her departure is felt as the loss of a friend of inestimable value.

The last time that Elizabeth left her house, for a public service, was to be present at a quarterly tea meeting, which was held at her much loved spot, Garrison Lane Chapel, by the members of the church dwelling in that neighbourhood, with a view to promote their brotherly love, and to enjoy more perfectly "the communion of saints." As her parents had removed further from the chapel, of course it was impossible for her to walk; her friends, therefore, procured a vehicle to convey her to the scene of holy fellowship, which was soon to he exchanged for the higher and more perfect fellowship of the church triumphant. For some time prior to her death, she had been staying with her friend, Mr Derrington, but finding herself getting worse, she wished to be removed to her own dwelling. It was however with great difficulty she accomplished the object of her desire, in consequence of her extreme weakness. A kind of Bath chair was procured, and she was drawn home in it, but was obliged to stop many times by the way, to recover from her pain and fatigue, before she could proceed. This was on the Friday, and early on Sunday morning, July 10, she left an earthly Sabbath, to enter on that rest which remaineth for the people of God. It does not appear from any remarks she made that she anticipated so soon to be removed, and therefore said nothing about her decease: for this however, she was always ready. In default of death-bed expressions, we must refer to the holy, consistent, and blameless tenor of her life. What an exchange was made by her emancipated spirit in that moment when it escaped from the little, inconvenient, and unsightly habitation in which it dwelt on earth, into the glorious and boundless regions of immortality. It was sown in weakness, it shall be raised in power; it was sown in dishonour, it shall be raised in glory; it was sown a natural body, it shall be raised a spiritual body.

It was not to be expected that such an individual would be carried to her grave unattended or unlamented by her numerous Christian friends. She was interred in the General Cemetery, and although this is situated between two or three miles from the spot where she died, she was followed by a procession which would have graced and honoured the remains of a person of wealth or rank. Her beloved friend Mr Derrington, and her class of Sunday scholars, preceded the corpse, which was borne by a company of the male teachers, and accompanied by the female teachers in mourning, who felt a melancholy pleasure in paying this last tribute of respect to one whom they tenderly loved, and justly esteemed. Her aged and venerable father and mother followed as mourners. In addition, a crowd of her neighbours and fellow-members joined the procession. Her pastor conducted the funeral service; and frequently as he has had to perform the same mournful duties in that beautiful cemetery, he can truly say he never saw such a multitude there as stood around the opened grave of this honoured member of his church; nor did he ever see so many tears fall, as dropped, when her little, infirm body was laid in its lowly bed of death to wait the raptures of the waking morn.

Many who visit that picturesque burying place, will pass by the sculptured tombs, and flattering memorials of the rich and the great, to stand upon the spot where reposes all that was mortal of Elizabeth Bales. She deserved as an appropriate epitaph, "She did what she could." Elizabeth departed, as we should be ready to say, too soon for the completion of her felicity upon earth; inasmuch as she did not live to witness the commencement of the erection of the second new chapel in her neighbourhood. This undertaking had been long delayed by obstacles which could not be overcome; at length, however, a prospect was presented of its being accomplished, and ground was purchased within about fifty yards of the dwelling in which her parents formerly resided, but from which they had, as I have said, lately removed. The progress of the arrangements for the new building was watched by her with deep interest, and in consequence of some new and threatening difficulties with almost painful concern. When Mr Derrington visited her, one of the first and most anxious enquiries used to be about the new chapel: and when hope of its being built was uppermost, she would please herself with the idea that she might yet be strengthened to worship God again in his house, and for this purpose begged her parents to move back to their former neighbourhood, and to take a cottage near the sanctuary. But her desire was not granted her, for the foundation stone was not laid until three weeks after she had entered on her long sabbatic rest. How would she have exulted over the thronging multitudes who assembled to witness the ceremony of that moving occasion, and with what anticipations of still greater blessings for her vicinity, would she have beheld the scene. Perhaps she was there though we saw her not. It might have been permitted to her, for all we know, to be a spectator of a scene, which is doubtless to be traced in some measure, to the influence of her labours, and the fervour of her prayers.

I was much affected by an expression of her mother during a visit I paid to her since the death of this precious daughter. "Our house, sir, is now so solitary since Elizabeth is gone: during her life it was always full of company, as she had friends ever coming to see her: but now we seem to have nobody about us." This little incident shows in what estimation she was held, and how much attraction went forth from her humble dwelling.

And now, what is to be gathered from this short memoir.

I. We see in it a beautiful exemplification of the true nature and transcendent excellence of religion. Religion is not merely an outward observance of ceremonies, nor an attendance upon ordinances; these things are worth nothing in themselves, mere bodily exercise that profits nothing, and is of no acceptance with God, but as they spring from the inward principle of a renewed, holy, and humble mind. Religion begins in deep conviction of sin, a sense of our fallen and ruined state as exposed to the wrath of God in consequence of transgression; and then goes on in a simple faith in the gospel, leading to an entire, thankful, and peace-giving dependence on the blood and righteousness of Christ, for acceptance with God. From this faith there arises love to God, to his people, to his ways, and to holiness. In proportion as faith is felt, it makes its possessor humble, meek and benevolent; full of pity for man, and zeal for the glory of God. See, how all this was exemplified in Elizabeth Bales. Never was there a more pure and simple-minded creature; a more dutiful daughter; a more harmless and inoffensive being, than she was; and yet how did she confess and bewail her sinfulness in the sight of God; how entirely did she renounce all dependence upon her own good doings, and how exclusively did she rely upon the righteousness of Christ. Observe the holy virtues which clustered in her character; how profound was her humility; how gentle her demeanour; how striking her meekness; how uncomplaining her submission; how exemplary her patience; how exquisite her benevolence; how ardent her zeal; how tender her attachments; how intense her piety; and to crown all, how unmixed was all this with any spiritual pride, any sense of superiority, or any sanctimonious airs. Had she been a Roman Catholic, or a Mystic, superstition would have invested this union of personal deformity and eminent piety, of usefulness and trance-like hallucinations, with something of supernatural visitation. How much is there for all of us to learn and to copy. Her body and her soul were in striking contrast with each other.

But the peace-giving nature of piety is most strikingly set forth in this beautiful example. Elizabeth, amidst all her poverty, her personal appearance, and her sufferings, was happy. Many a girl of envied beauty, dwelling amidst the splendours of wealth, enjoying rank herself, and flattered and caressed by those still greater, might, on account of the untroubled flow of her thoughts, and the quiet, lake-like, heaven-reflecting surface of her heart, have looked with envy upon the little decrepit form that pursued its daily rounds of mercy, panting for breath, in the neighbourhood of Garrison Lane Chapel. She looked happy, for she felt so. Notes of praise and not of complaint were ever flowing from her lips. Many heard her expressions of gratitude, none ever had to expostulate with her on a murmuring expression.

And now contemplate the elevating nature of religion. How entirely did moral and spiritual excellence raise her above all disadvantages of person and station, and cover with its lustre her deformity and poverty. What would she have been without religion? An object of pity to the good, and of ridicule to the bad, but of respect or interest to none. She would have lived without comfort and without esteem. It was this divine excellence that in spite of all that was repulsive to the bodily eye, made her an object of regard to all that knew her. Yes, and this did so raise her, that half the women who have passed through society, with all the advantages of beauty, elegance, and wealth in their favour, whatever they may have had of admiration and of flattery, have had far less of love and of esteem, than this child of poverty and sorrow. So true is the language of God, "Since thou wast precious in my sight, thou hast been honourable."

II. What a proof is this narrative of the common remark, that where there is a heart to do good, there is an opportunity; where there is a will there is a way to be useful, and that no disadvantages and obstacles are so great as to be insurmountable to an intelligent and determined zeal. If with that little deformed person, if with the feebleness of constitution which it produced, and with poverty of circumstances in addition, Elizabeth could do so much good by direct personal effort, what might not be done by others, to whom these disadvantages do not belong? Alas! how much less good do any of us do, than we might: and if she lamented over the little work she did for Christ, with how much greater shame and grief should we deplore our unfruitfulness? How shall we excuse ourselves for our indolence? What defence shall we set up? The world is perishing around us.

Sinners are going down to the pit before our eyes. Immortal souls by countless millions are crowding to the regions of eternal despair: how do we answer the charge that we do not do more for their salvation? How little are we affected by the terrific scene! How little are we penetrated by a sense of the ignorance, sin and misery which appeal to our own senses! Oh where is the constraining love of Christ? Where the compassion for souls? Where the sense of responsibility to God? All may do good, and all should do it. There needs not the sex and strength of the man: women may do good; there needs not personal advantage: decrepitude may do good; there needs not wealth: poverty may do good. This blessed luxury is within the reach of all, and to have no appetite or taste for it is but too plain an indication of a wrong state of soul. In this world of sin and sorrow, where our purest enjoyments are so mixed, there is no bliss equal to that which is derived from the exercise of benevolence. There is a very admirable tract published by the Religious Tract Society entitled, *How to Do Good*, or *Ways of Caring for the Souls of Others*, which enumerates the following methods of pious zeal. You can pray for your families, friends, neighbours, and the world. You can set a holy example, and show that religion makes you holy, kind, gentle, good-tempered, and happy. You can speak to your families, friends, and neighbours, about their souls. When you see people do or say wrong, you can kindly speak to them. You can read the Bible, and pray with your families. You can lend and give tracts. You can read the Bible and good books to those who will listen. You can teach others to read. Some of you can be Sunday School teachers. You can give financially to support societies for spreading the gospel. You can urge people to go to God's house. You can visit the sick. You can send your children to a Sunday School, or invite others to send theirs. You can speak to your companions about religion. You can urge people to keep the Sabbath holy. You can be kind to others, and then they will be more likely to listen to what you say. You can write letters to your friends, and try to do them good, and ask them to do good to others. When you are going to the house of God, you can speak to those whom you see sinning. In walking along the road, or anywhere else, you can often drop a word to other people. In coaches, steamers, and other places, you can speak to people. When you have a few minutes to spare, you can visit some neighbours, and speak to them about their souls. Here are twenty ways of doing good. The tract which enumerates them, gives instances of success with most of them. Harlan Page was a man who loved to do good, and between the hours of his work, he went and spoke to others about their souls, besides other ways of doing good, and he was the means of turning more than a hundred people to God, some of whom were afterwards ministers.

III. What a lesson is here taught to the poor. Much are they to be pitied. None can fully know the ills of poverty by observation. Experience alone can give this knowledge. But still it cannot be denied that these are always increased by sin, and diminished by piety. Religion is the best antidote of poverty: it has in ten thousand instances prevented it, and in ten thousand more alleviated it. Who can be poorer than was Elizabeth? For years she lived almost entirely upon the bounty of others: yet who more happy, respectable, or useful? Let the poor read her history and learn that happiness may be found in a cottage. "A man's life," said our Lord, "consisteth not in the abundance of the things that he hath." True blessedness comes from spiritual things, not from temporal ones. "Hearken, my beloved brethren, hath not God chosen the poor of this world rich in faith and heirs of the kingdom which he hath promised to them that love him?" Such are the accents which Christianity floats in heavenly music over the humble vale of poverty. "Rich in faith." This may mean either that faith is the best, the true riches, a blessed truth, for if it were ponderable we should say a grain of faith is better than a ton of gold: it gives an interest in all the unsearchable riches of Christ, of grace, and of glory; it justifies, sanctifies, saves: or it may signify that the faith of the poor is peculiarly strong: yes, it is amidst the privations of poverty where the believer has nothing in hand and nothing in hope, but what he sees in the promise of God, that faith puts forth its mightiest power, and manifests its richest glories. Was not this exemplified in the case before us? What had Elizabeth to live upon but God's promise that she should not want? Her faith was rich and gloriously influential. And then see the other terms of this poor man's text: heirs! And to what an inheritance? Toil? Sorrow? Want? Yes, oftentimes: but of something else if he is a Christian;

"of God," "of salvation," "of a kingdom." He is a son of the King of Kings, and destined to wear a crown of life, *James 1:12;* to sit upon a throne, *Revelation 3:21;* and to reign for ever and ever in a kingdom, *2 Timothy 2:12.* Rejoice ye poor, all this is for you, if you are partakers of faith.

Religion will make you respectable. Who was more truly respectable than Elizabeth? Her poverty, her deformity, her dependence, detracted nothing from her moral worth, did not sink her in public estimation; or number her with the many who are treated with contempt and scorn. On the contrary, few, very few of far higher rank and station, have received more attention or respect. Ours is happily a country where moral worth is sure to find its proper level, where there is enough of morality and piety to estimate respectability more by character than by wealth. Many a rich man is despised, as he ought to be, on account of his vices; many a poor man is as much esteemed because of his virtues. I allow that something else besides piety is necessary to give true respectability to the poor, but it is all within their reach. I mean good sense, good manners, and good temper. Let a man have all these and no one will pass his door or himself with contempt. With religion as the substance, and general good conduct as the polish, the poor man is a gem which all judges of excellence will know how to value, and be sure to admire, though the setting be in copper instead of gold. Take comfort my poor friends, if you answer to this description you are not undervalued by those who know you; God respects you, Christ respects you, angels respect you, good men respect you, bad men respect you, many that seem to despise you, really esteem you. Be assured that goodness is respectability, whether it live in a mansion or a cottage, whether it wear satin or cotton, whether it feed upon venison or a crust.

Nor are you, though poor, shut out from doing good, any more than you are from being good. O! if you have a heart to be useful, you may find abundant opportunities to employ your energies. Instances might be cited without number, if it were necessary, of people in the humblest walks of life doing great good; and that not only by all kinds of ingenious devices, but in the way of direct effort. Take the two following as specimens. There was a member of the church under my care, who lived in an almshouse, and was so distorted by rheumatism as to be quite a cripple, and unable to walk or stand; and in addition, as a result of the disease, her fingers were twisted into all kinds of shapes. On entering her apartment one day I found her with some religious tracts. "Well Mrs H___," said I, "What are you doing?" "O sir," she replied, "I am sorting my tracts." "What for?" "To send out to my neighbours." The fact was that she received these tracts from richer friends from time to time, and then employed someone to carry them round the spacious court of almshouses in which she lived, and other dwellings in the neighbourhood; and her work was to keep up a regular supply and exchange. Thus poor old Ellen in the almshouse could find some way to be useful. To give one more instance; I was visiting a brother minister a few years ago with a view to assist him in a missionary meeting, which was to be held in his chapel. While I was in his house he called me into the kitchen, for what purpose I did not know until the scene explained itself. There stood an aged woman about eighty years old talking with the minister, and looking, (with a smiling countenance, and with sparkling eyes, as far as such aged orbs could sparkle,) upon some silver which my friend at that moment held in the palm of his hand. It might have been supposed she was going to receive this money to increase her comfort, for all her income was half-a-crown a week from the parish, and what the kindness of her friends might occasionally bestow, and out of this she paid eighteen pence for her lodging; but no, she came to give, not to receive. That money, amounting to more than ten shillings, she had earned by knitting various articles and selling them; and she was then in the kitchen, where I saw her, to place it in the hand of her minister for the missionary society. So you see the poor can do something for God's cause, if they have "a mind to work." But they may also do much in the way of direct effort for the conversion of souls. Can they not warn a profane sinner, or explain the way of salvation to those that are ignorant and out of the way, or distribute tracts, and talk about their contents, or invite the neglecters of public worship to the house of God? Let the poor understand, value, and enjoy their privilege.

IV. Is there not a word for the rich from Elizabeth's memoir? Can they learn nothing from this chapter of the humble annals of the poor? Should this little book meet the eye of any whom Providence has blessed with wealth, station and influence, I would say to them, Does your piety flourish amidst the comforts and the elegances of life as hers did in the cottage of poverty? Must you not admit that if you are richer in money, she was richer in faith? Learn to think less and less of the wealth of this world, and more and more of the unsearchable riches of Christ. Lower the estimate which pride and vanity form of the importance of worldly distinctions. "Let the brother of low degree rejoice in that he is exalted; but the rich in that he is made low: because as the flower of the grass he shall pass away. For the sun is no sooner risen with a burning heat, but it withereth the grass, and the flower thereof falleth, and the grace of the fashion of it perisheth: so also shall the rich man fade away in his ways." How many rich professors are far less happy now than was this daughter of poverty and affliction; and oh! how much below her will they be in that world where the degrees of glory will be in proportion, not to the amount of wealth, but to the degrees of grace! How much would the rich learn were they more frequently to visit the dwellings of the poor, and see how contented and peaceful those of them that are pious are, amidst all their privations! The well-known anecdote of poor Mary is so much in point here, that I cannot omit it. She had a rich neighbour who was of a querulous temper, and found only cause for complaint, where multitudes would have only found matter of thankfulness. One day, on returning from the chapel where she had been worshipping God, this lady overtook Mary, who frequented the same place, and who was well known to her. She entered into conversation, and as usual, had many causes of complaint. Mary, who was a woman of good sense as well as piety, endeavoured to lead her mind away from her sorrows to her mercies. When they arrived opposite her door, she respectfully asked her wealthy neighbour to walk in, and then leading her to her empty cupboard opened it, with the question, "Do you see anything there, Ma'am?" "Nothing," was the reply. And opening a drawer or two that contained her scanty wardrobe, repeated the question, "What do you see there?" "Very little." "Then you see all I have in the world: but why should I be anxious, who have God for my Father, Christ for my Saviour, salvation for my portion, and heaven for my home?" The lady felt the rebuke so wisely and so respectfully given, and found grace to profit by it.

And then what a lesson to the rich as regards their usefulness. O did but the wealthy know their opportunity, and feel their obligations, and appreciate their privileges, to bless their fellow-men, how happy might they be themselves, and how happy might they make others! It is a distressing spectacle in such a world as ours, where evil of every kind so much abounds, to observe the disgusting and odious selfishness of many of the rich, who are wholly taken up with their own luxurious gratification, as if born only to pamper their appetites and indulge their tastes, without bestowing a thought or a care upon the misery that prevails around them. Can they wonder at the envy, suspicion, ill-will, and hatred of the poor? Can they be astonished at the sullen murmurs and convulsive heavings of that mass of wretchedness in which they have left the principles of infidelity and sedition to be scattered by the spirits of mischief, unresisted and unchecked by kindness, liberality and religious effort? Whatever are the vices of the poor, they are deeply conscious of kindness, and alive to the feelings of gratitude. More of the oil of benevolence poured over the waves of discontent and disaffection would have a mighty influence in calming the troubled surface. Especially let the rich who make a profession of religion remember their obligations. Let it be their hallowed ambition, their constant study, and rich enjoyment, to find how much good they can do. Let them win for themselves, – and it is a precious prize, – the widow's tear of gratitude, the blessing of him that was ready to perish, the thanks unutterable of souls saved by their instrumentality, and the testimony of their approving Saviour. Few, very few, of the wealthier members of the flock of Christ are yet exerting themselves as they ought to do. Few indeed like the subject of this memoir, "go about doing good." Their liberality and usefulness are rather a composition and a compromise to be let alone than an actual engagement in the service of our Lord. True it is, Elizabeth had few duties and few occupations: benevolent activity was a relief from what would otherwise have been an oppressive solitude: and after all it is, I allow, a loftier course of mercy, a nobler stretch of costly and disinterested goodness, to sacrifice the hours which might be devoted to innocent recreations, and to elegant ease: to take something from the profits of business, the pleasures of friendship, or the soft enjoyments and engrossing demands of domestic scenes, and offer this contribution to the good of others. Happy in time, happier still in eternity, will those be, who thus exhibit the mind that was in Christ.

And is there no lesson for females? What when the interesting subject of this memoir was of that class? Your sex, my female friends, stands with honour on the page of every history under heaven, and especially of that one which is written by the inspiration of God. The same blessed page which proclaims your dishonour in the sin of your first mother, displays the glorious part you are to bear in the instrumentality of saving a lost world; and many successive chapters of the sacred volume accumulate the testimonies and the evidence of your usefulness. A useless woman, a selfish woman, an unfeeling woman, is a sin against her sex, formed as it was for sympathy and mercy, and is a sin also against the history of her sex. Be active, my sisters, be active. You are far more so than your fathers, husbands, and brothers. You outstrip us in zeal and in piety too: still last at the cross, first at the sepulchre, oftenest at the sanctuary, longest at the throne of grace, busiest in the house of sorrow: go on, value and maintain your distinction, and especially maintain it with that profound modesty which is the ornament of your excellence, and reveals while it conceals, genuine worth. Elizabeth with all her activity was singularly retiring in her deportment, and unobtrusive in her demeanour. It was the activity of principle, not of passion merely; the constraint of redeeming love, which, like its Divine source, did not cry nor lift up its voice in the street. There is danger in this age of female activity of some loss of female modesty; especially of young women becoming forward, obtrusive, and bold: thus it is that weeds grow with the flowers, weaken their strength, hide their beauty, and corrupt their fragrance. Be watchful. Let not your good be evil spoken of. Resemble as much as possible, not "the sisters of charity," who though noiseless, attract attention by their garb and their order, but those blessed angels who minister to the heirs of salvation, and who perform their embassies unseen and unheard.

Tract distributors and visitors of the sick, behold a model which you may imitate with great advantage. Elizabeth's work in this department of her labour was at once her business and her delight. She went to it as a vocation, and pursued it with a steadiness, produced by the double stimulus of conscience and affection. Her tracts were not thrown in at the door, as if, like the distributors of hand bills, she had so many to give away, and the sooner that the last was gone, no matter how, the better: to her they were means of introduction for herself, little harbingers to prepare her own way to go in, and sit down, and talk with her neighbours about their souls. And this is the way to do good. A good tract distributor needs more than a foot and a hand: she should have an eye beaming with affection, lips on which is the law of kindness, and a tongue the accents of which are instruction, warning, and consolation to the ignorant, wicked, and wretched. Tracts are now happily become very common; so common that in many cases they are received with indifference, where they are not, as in some cases they are, surlily refused; this makes it the more necessary to converse and explain them, and in some cases to read them. Great skill and tact are necessary to gain ready access to the houses and hearts of the poor on such errands, but the secret of doing so is love and gentleness. Elizabeth in many instances conquered by affection. She never resented rudeness, was never petulant, but by the meek and quiet manner in which she bore with unkindness, in the few cases in which she met with it, subdued and softened the individual that expressed it. A temper, the serenity of which is with difficulty ruffled by opposition and rudeness, is essential to a visitor of the poor, who goes to reclaim them from sin. The sweet persuasiveness of her manner often served her in dealing with the sceptic and the scoffer instead of argument; for it is willingly conceded that she could more powerfully recommend religion by describing its blessedness, than prove its divine authority by argument, or answer the objections of the cavilling disputant. She was herself with such men an argument of greater weight than the logic of others. Still, it is desirable in this age, when infidelity has become condescending, and leaving the heights of society has descended into the vale of poverty, that tract distributors should know how to answer the objections of infidels, and how to prove the divine claims of the religion they are anxious to spread.

Happily the merciful spirit of Christianity is also seen in this age, not only in sending missionaries to distant lands, but in the various benevolent institutions, for visiting and relieving the sick in our own. Many, like our deceased friend, go to the chamber of affliction, and to the bedside of disease, to impart the medicine of the soul, in words whereby men may be comforted and saved. Let no one venture upon such an errand without tenderness of spirit and gentleness of manner. Elizabeth was a pattern in a sick chamber, so soft in voice, so gentle in manner, so tender in spirit, though perhaps a little too prone, from the very longing of her soul after the salvation of those she visited, to believe they were saved. I know no office so difficult as to the discharge of its duties, as the visitation of the sick; and with the exception of cases of chronic disease, which leaves the mind long at leisure to think and meditate and pray, I do not anticipate so much real good from visits of this kind as many do. Religion is a mental process from beginning to end, and the man half delirious with fever, in a state of extreme prostration of strength, or writhing in agony, can attend but little to the words of instruction. It were well to take the people off as much as possible, from a kind of superstitious regard to, and dependence upon the prayers of a minister, or pious people, in sickness, and lead them to consider that life and health are the time to seek the salvation of the soul. Still there are innumerable cases to which these remarks do not apply, but in which, during the slow waste of consumption and other diseases, the soul has leisure to think of her dark and winding course, and opportunity to return to God: and in which the voice of the friendly visitor is essentially necessary. Ministers can do but little alone for such instances, and may be materially assisted by such gentle spirits as have been described in this memoir. As a general remark, it may be said that much Christian intelligence, as well as much kindness of heart, and gentleness of manner, are necessary for such an office; and also a very clear, discriminating, simple method of stating the ground of a sinner's hope towards God.

And now I devote a few pages in conclusion, and with great earnestness, to that useful and honourable class to which Elizabeth especially belonged, I mean the Sunday School teachers. It is in this character I wish you to contemplate her, and in which she really is so bright a pattern.

I will not conceal the concern which I have sometimes felt, lest you, my dear friends, should be in any measure injured by the manner in which you have been often appealed to of late, and in which the importance of your useful labours has been described. It is indeed true that your office is important, and its duties of momentous consequence to the well-being of those who are the objects of your kind attention, for you have to do not only with thinking minds, but with immortal souls, and your object is not only to train the rational, but the immortal creature. Nothing, of course, can be more momentous than eternity, and it is to eternity that your labours relate: but, in proportion to the grandeur of your object, and the loftiness of your aim, there is a danger of your having the feeling of vanity elicited by descriptions of your work, and calculations and statements of your numbers. The latter idea gives a sense of importance in any cause. Many an individual who is quite humble in his state of isolation, and when he labours on amidst his own difficult duties, and his consciousness of imperfection, still feels something of pride or vanity when he calculates the number of his associates: his mind expands to the limits of the vast circle in which he moves. Beware, then, of the pride of aggregation, and suffer nothing to corrupt the deep humility of your spirit.

In the beautiful instance which I have set before you in this brief memoir, you have seen a just conception formed of the ultimate object of Sunday School teaching. Elizabeth never for a moment forgot that her children had immortal souls; that those souls were lost by sin; that Christ had died for their salvation; and that her business was to seek their conversion from the error of their ways, and save them from death. This is the true light in which to view the subject. There is as much of philosophy in this, as there is of piety: for in seeking the greater good, we seek all the lesser ones contained within it. You want to fit your children, or you ought to do so, for all the stations they may be called to occupy in future life; and the best way to do this is to endeavour to bring them under the influence of religion. I beseech you to remember that you have to do with souls. Ponder the worth of a soul. Weigh the awful import of that word, *damnation*. Measure, if you can, the height of salvation. Yearn for souls. What would you not do to save your children from falling into the water, or the fire. Think of the bottomless pit, and the fire that is never quenched. Take a proper aim in all you do. Look as high as heaven, as deep as to the mouth of hell, and as far as eternity.

For such an object qualify yourself well, by a large measure of mental improvement. Make yourself well acquainted with the powers of the human mind, and the best method of training them; especially the means of fixing the volatile attention of youth, and of exciting a thirst after knowledge and self-improvement in your young charges. But above all cultivate a habit of devotional feeling. Remember that piety is as truly the first qualification of a good Sunday School teacher, as it is of a good minister. Catch the fervent piety of Elizabeth. Imitate her devotional habits, her meditative, prayerful spirit. She was eminently a woman of prayer. Her mother often found her fainted on her knees. The intensity of her devotion, and the greatness of her labours exhausted her weak frame. Our Sunday Schools should be the very atmosphere of religion. The children should be made to feel that in the presence of their teacher they are standing before an embodied form of living godliness. You cannot seek the salvation of the souls of others, if you are not alive to your own. Ask the question, are you in earnest for eternity? Are you fleeing from the wrath to come? Are you walking with God, living a life of faith, prayer, watchfulness, and holiness? Oh, you will make a poor Sunday School teacher without this.

Mark the devotedness of Elizabeth. Her soul, her whole soul, was in her work: it was her meat and her drink; her life was bound up in it. We can do nothing well, which we do not do in earnest. "Whatsoever thy hand findeth to do, do it with thy might." Those who carry to the school only half a heart, will do nothing. They had better stay away; they only keep out others who would do far better than themselves. All our schools have some such, who are hindrances, not helps. Lukewarmness is not only in its results inefficient, but makes the work disagreeable. It is impossible to enjoy what is done in such a manner. It is all mere drudgery, and is very irksome. Zeal is pleasure: it is the vital glow and energy of a healthy and active mind. It is good to be always zealous in this good thing. Watch, labour, teach, pray, as one in earnest. Be constant, and lose no opportunity. Be punctual and lose not a moment. Eternity hangs upon every instant. Let no measure of duty satisfy you. Adopt your children as objects of interest and affection. Follow them to their houses; know all about them. Thus acquire an influence over them. If teachers have no influence over their children; if the children are rude, refractory, insubordinate, in a school where order is generally observed, the teacher is unfit for his office. The disorderly state of his class proclaims his incompetency, unless there be some counteracting cause over which he has no control. If Elizabeth, notwithstanding her deformity, poverty and weakness, could by her love, and gentleness, and devotedness, keep her children in such order, who need despair of doing it, if proper means were used? Love, system, mildness, devotedness, patience, will tame a savage. Lions and elephants are tamed by love and firmness; for love is a language which brutes understand; a law which they are willing to obey.

Conciliate the affection and secure the esteem of your fellow teachers. What a pattern of this excellence is before you. She was never known to quarrel with a single teacher. She loved all, and by all was beloved. Her kindness to others brought back kindness to herself. To her influence might, in some measure, be attributed the uninterrupted harmony which pervaded the school. She kept peace, and therefore had never to make it; and prevented breaches, which is far easier than to repair them. A good teacher is ever a peaceable one. He neither raises a faction nor joins one. He has no ear for murmurs or complaints, except it be to hush them; and never blows the coals of discord, nor waters the root of bitterness. What mischief might one discontented and turbulent teacher do in a school, where there are other inflammable spirits, ready to take fire from his own! The putrid fever of disaffection is as contagious as it is malignant. Keep clear from the disease and neither communicate nor receive it.

Imitate also the untiring patience, the unwearied zeal of this estimable woman. Nothing but the hand of disease arrested her, and when kept by that from the school-room she used to have her class occasionally in her own chamber. Hers was a service of nearly twenty years, and she loved her work to the last. Had she lived until she was seventy, she would still have been a Sunday School teacher. Be not weary in well-doing. Amidst many who soon tire and faint, be it your ambition to see how many of these your zeal can outlive. What an honour is it to have it said, "There is a teacher of twenty years' standing."

Like Elizabeth, be attached to your ministers, and be ever willing to consult them, and to follow their counsels. How devoted was she to the comfort, how regardful of the peace, how concerned for the usefulness of the town missionary who laboured in the neighbourhood, and whom she considered as her minister. I believe she would have been almost willing to die rather than for one moment to have thrown an obstacle in the way of his useful ministrations, or to injure the prosperity of the congregation at Garrison Lane Chapel. Her labours, much as she loved them and delighted in them, were no separate and detached department, but part of a whole over which he presided. Her usefulness was a rivulet that flowed into the greater stream of his. She was his willing handmaid, and she looked up to him with a deference, which though not servile, was eminently respectful. It is this blessed harmony between the Sunday School teacher and pastor which I am most anxious to promote. I want our ministers to look with the tenderest interest, and with the most affectionate care on the labours of these their invaluable assistants; and them to look up without jealousy, and with unfeigned respect, to their minister's general, unobtrusive, and paternal superintendence. In him there should be nothing dictatorial, as if they were servants: in them nothing suspicious, as if he came among them to invade their prerogative. It is a delightful sight to behold a good understanding between a Christian pastor and a body of devoted teachers.

Remember, eternity is at hand, the bliss of which will be enhanced by the recollections of time. Our friend has experienced this already by meeting in glory some whom she was the honoured instrument of helping to raise from the privations of poverty to the felicities of immortality. Some harps, doubtless, are struck with a stronger hand in praise of our Lord, since she has arrived in heaven, for the instructions of her lips, the consistency of her example, or the fidelity of her reproofs. Sunday School teachers, go and do likewise; be stimulated, guided and encouraged by the example of Elizabeth Bales.